AWESOME ANIMALS

&

CREATURES of the SEA

COLORING BOOK

2 BOOK BUNDLE

AWESOME ANIMALS
Coloring Book

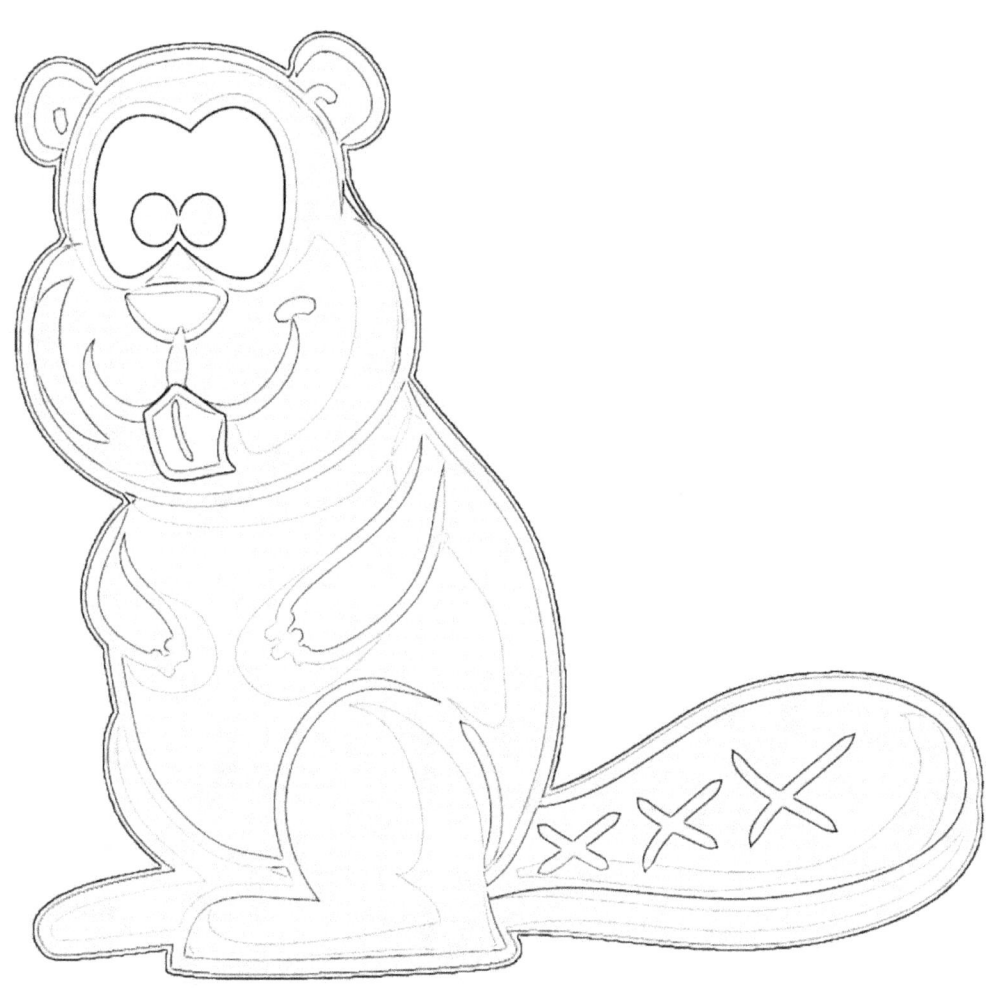

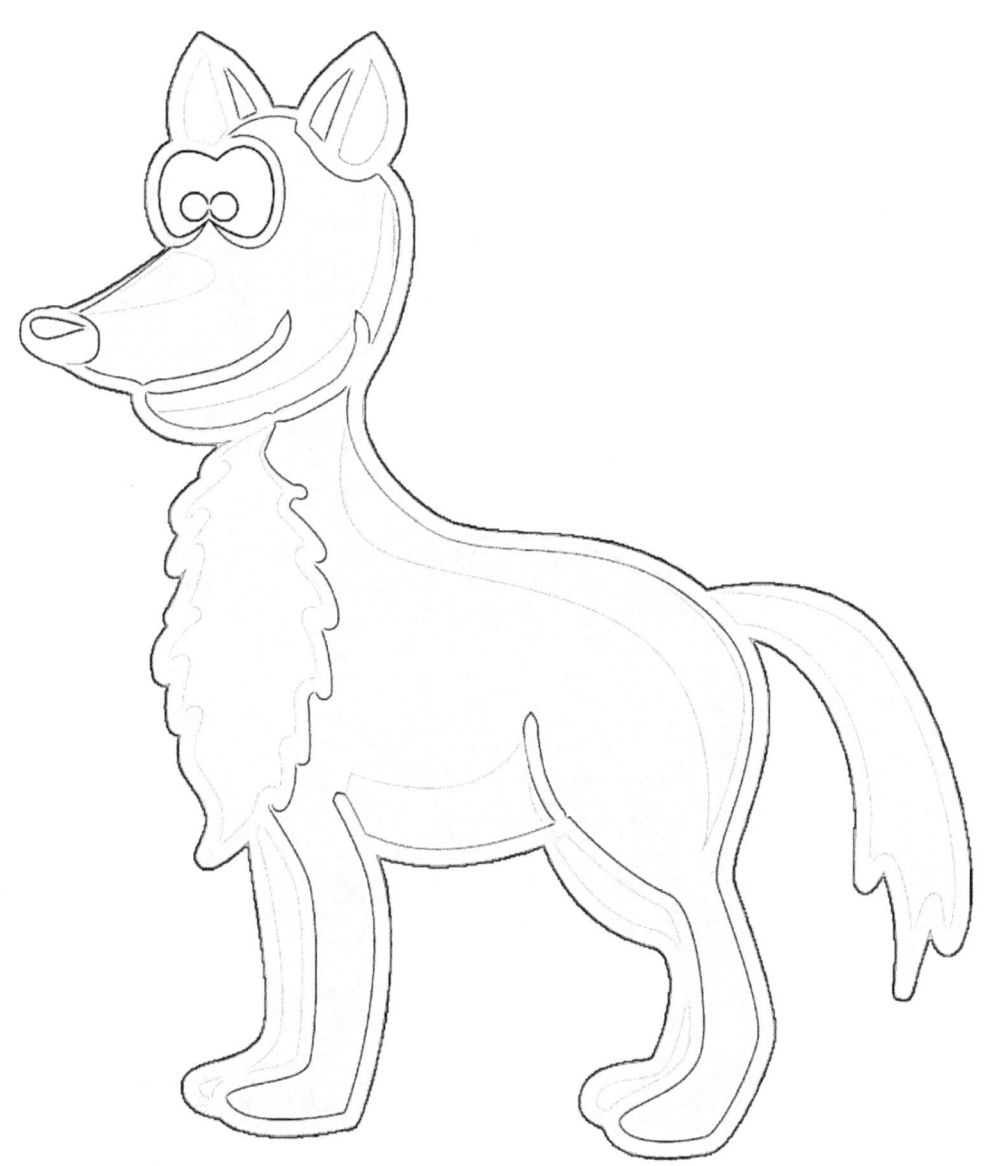

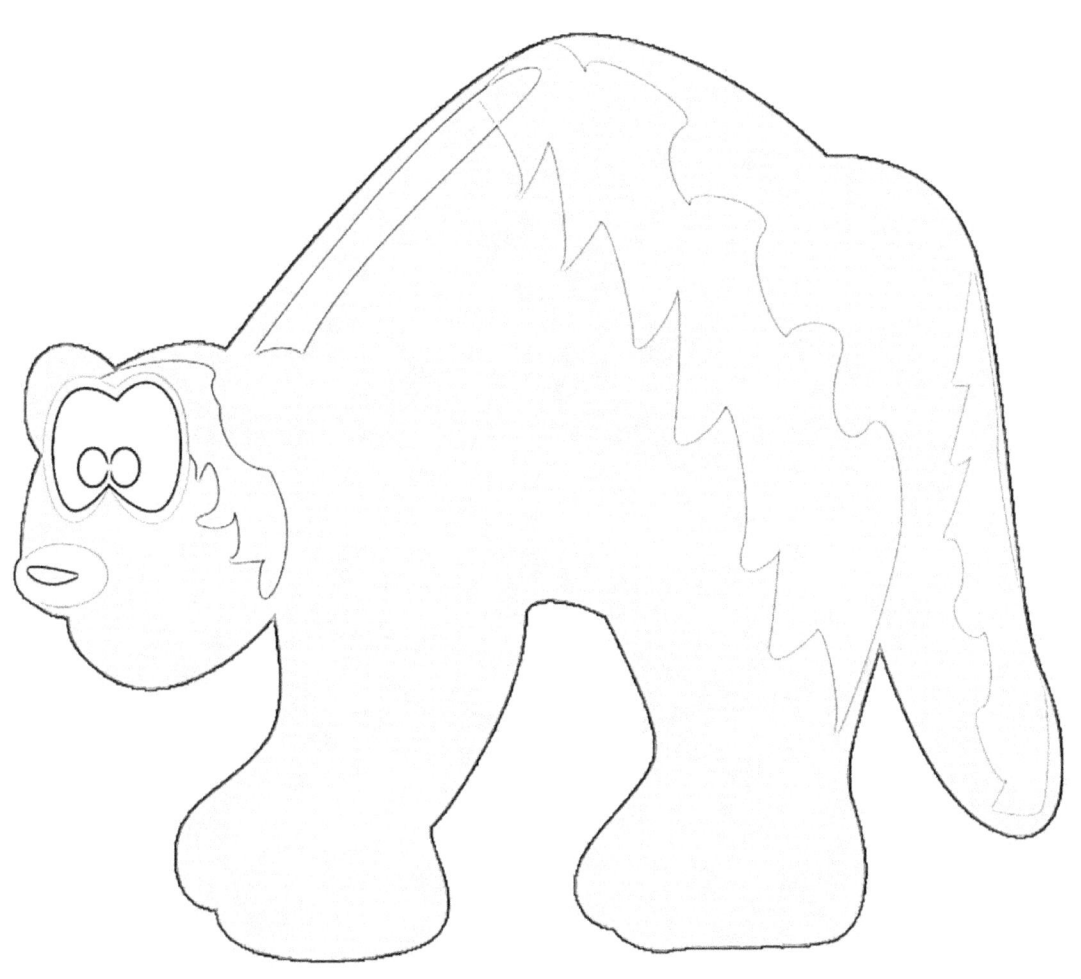

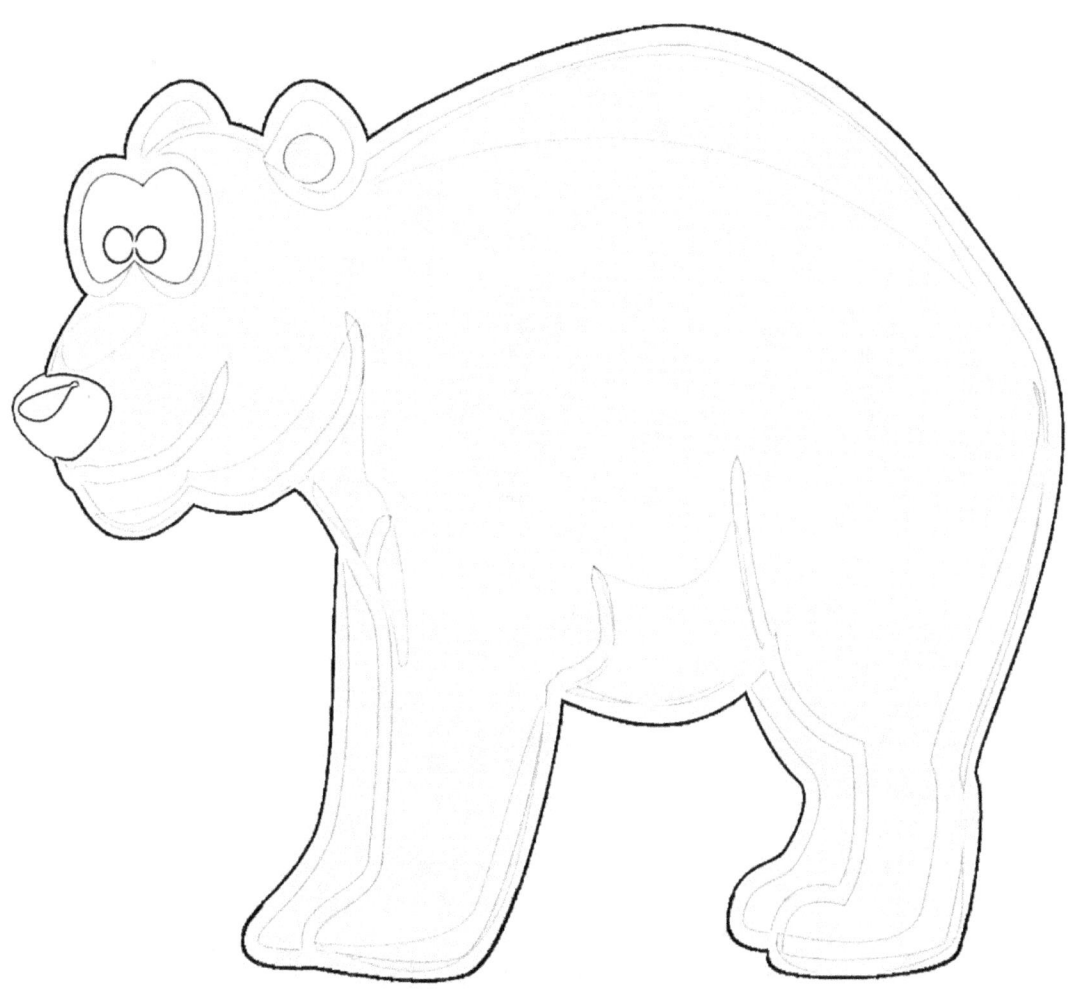

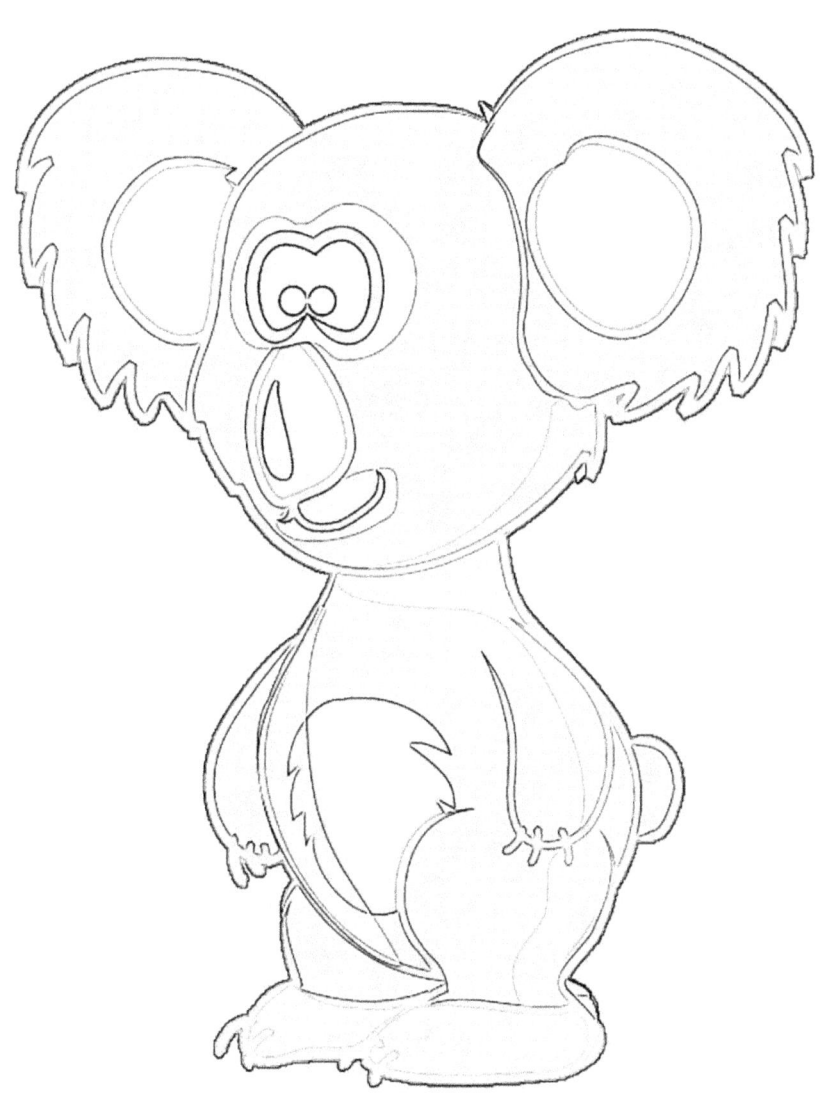

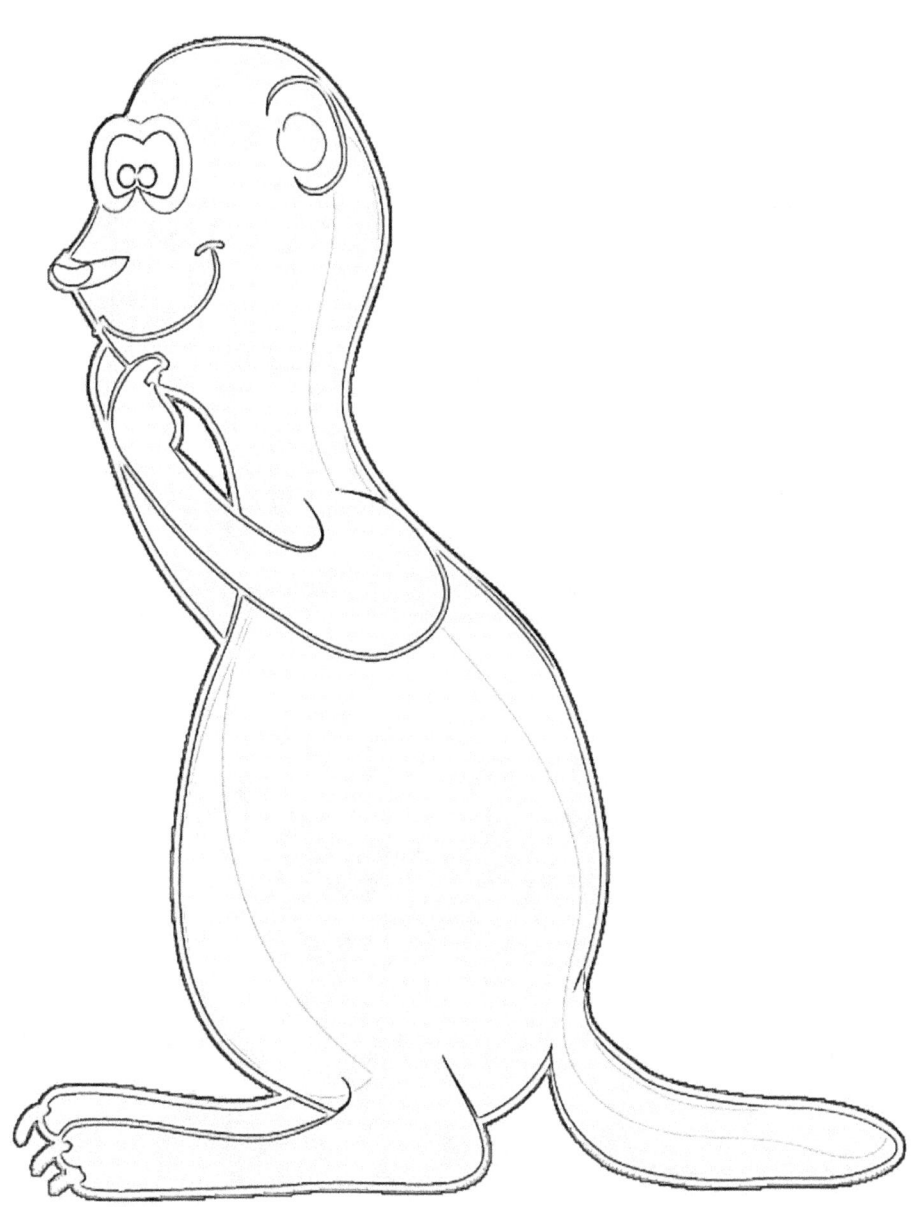

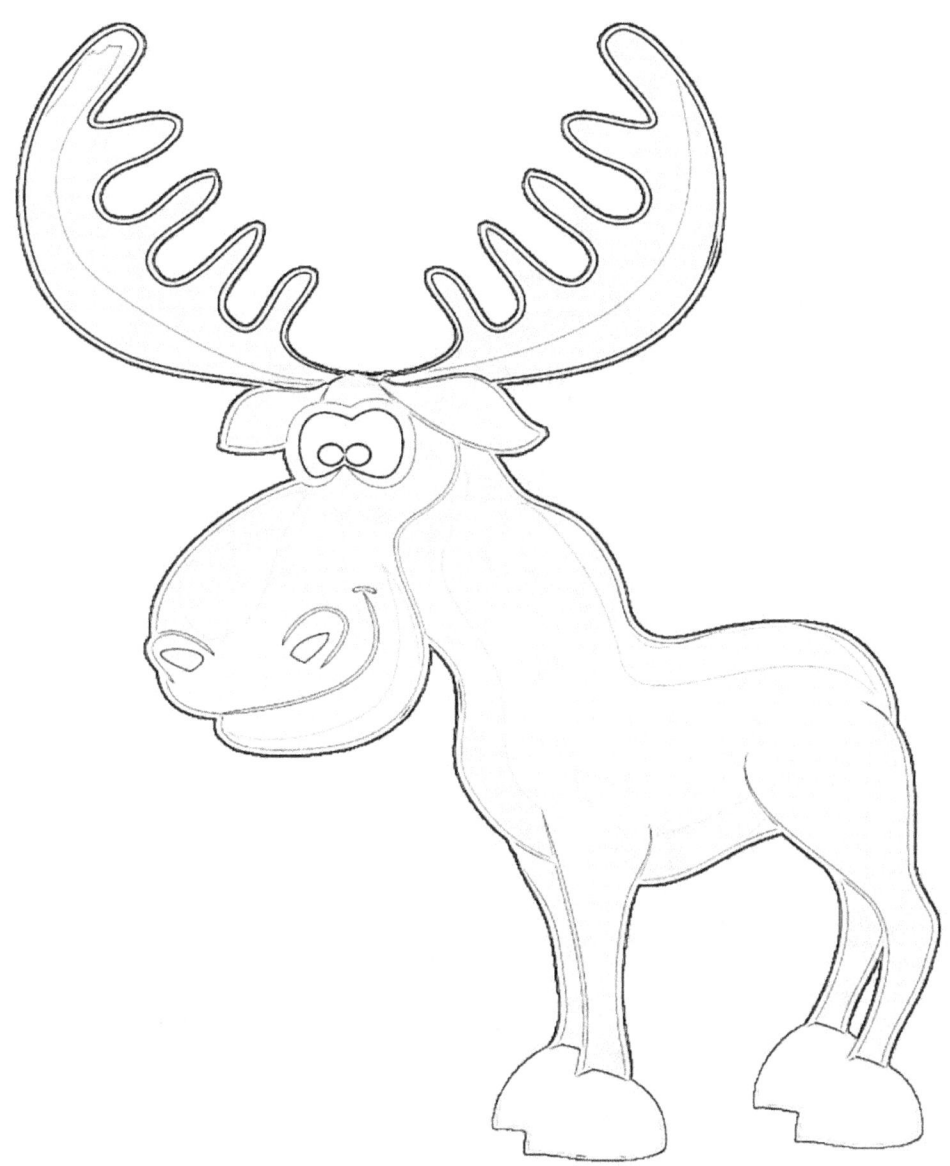

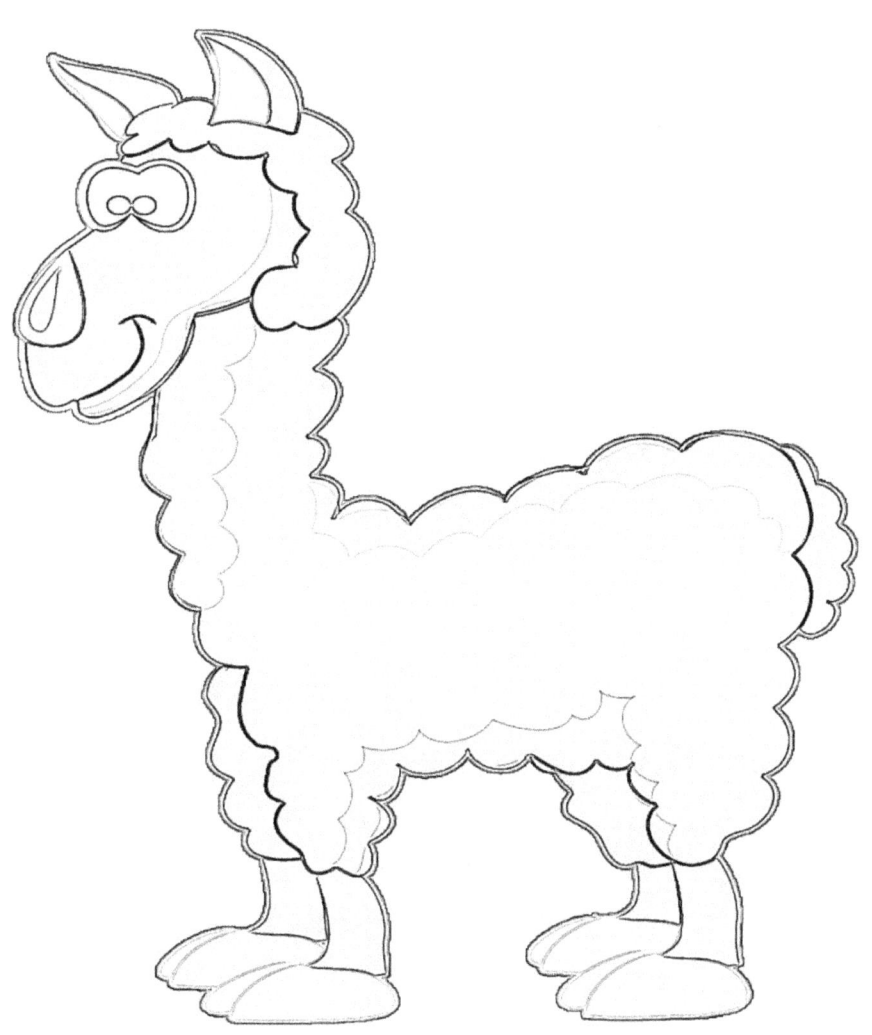

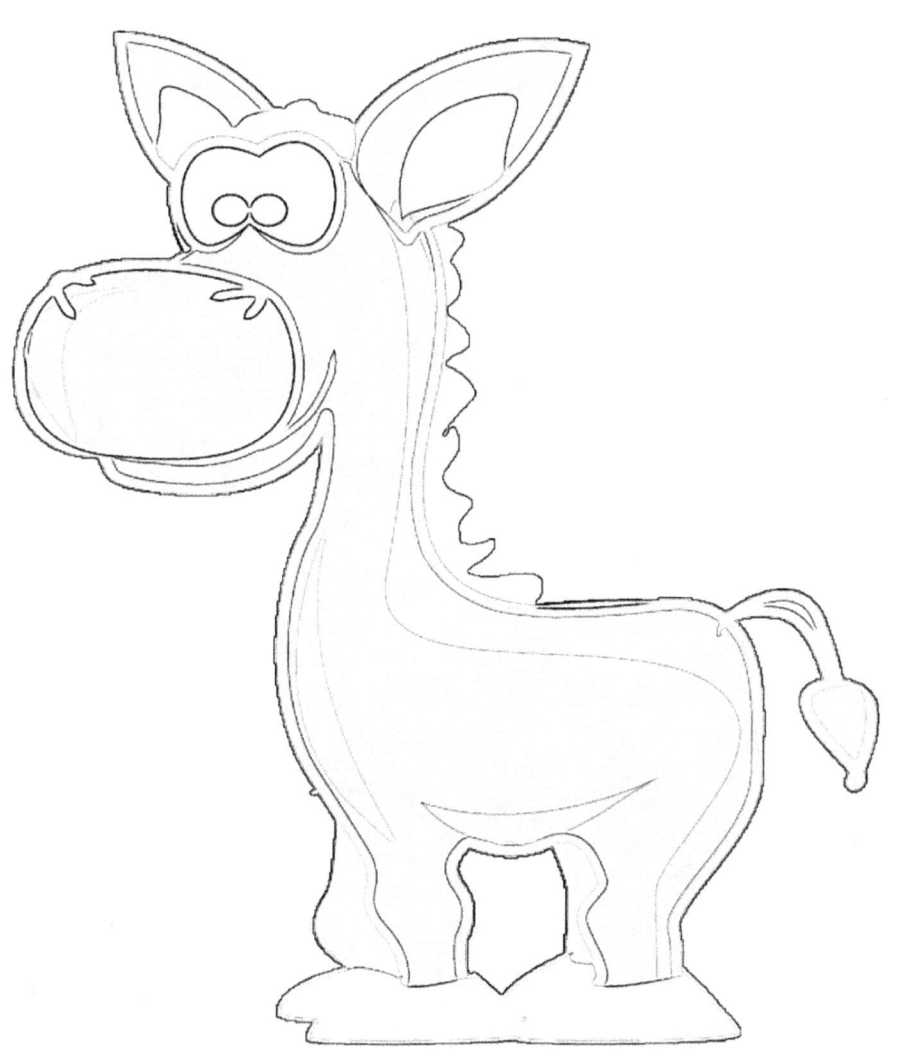

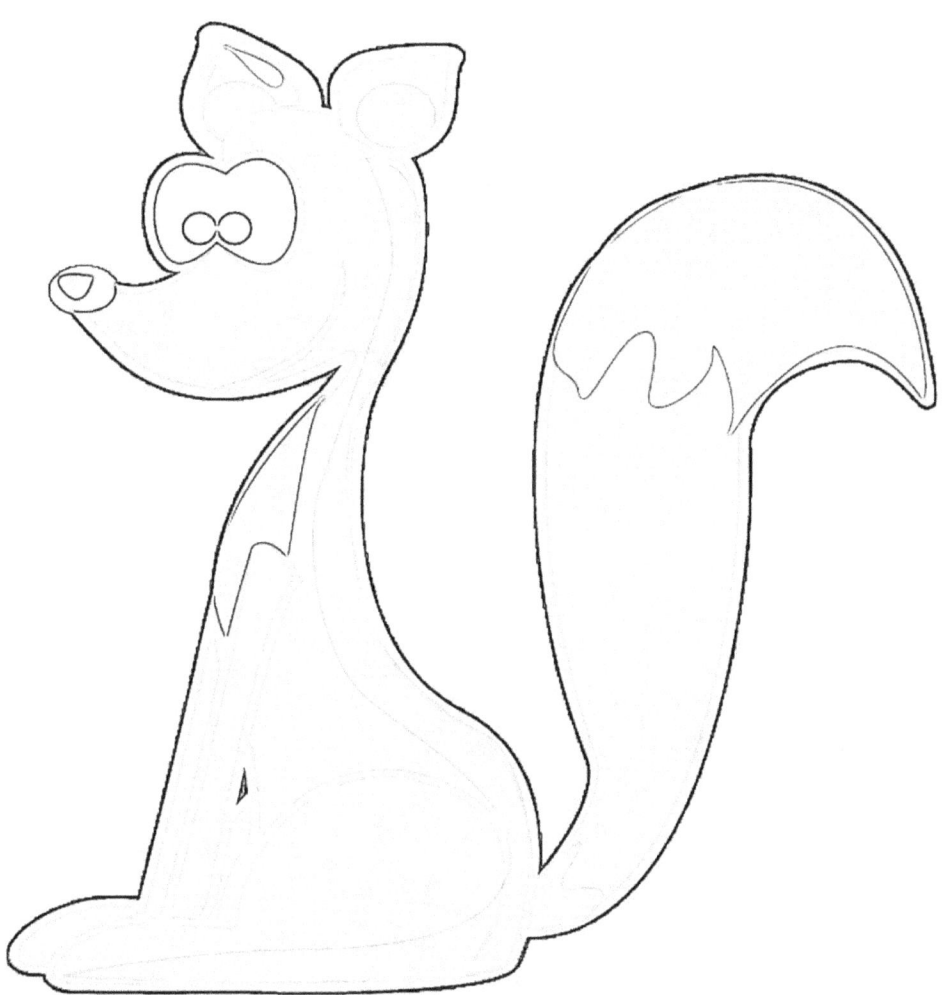

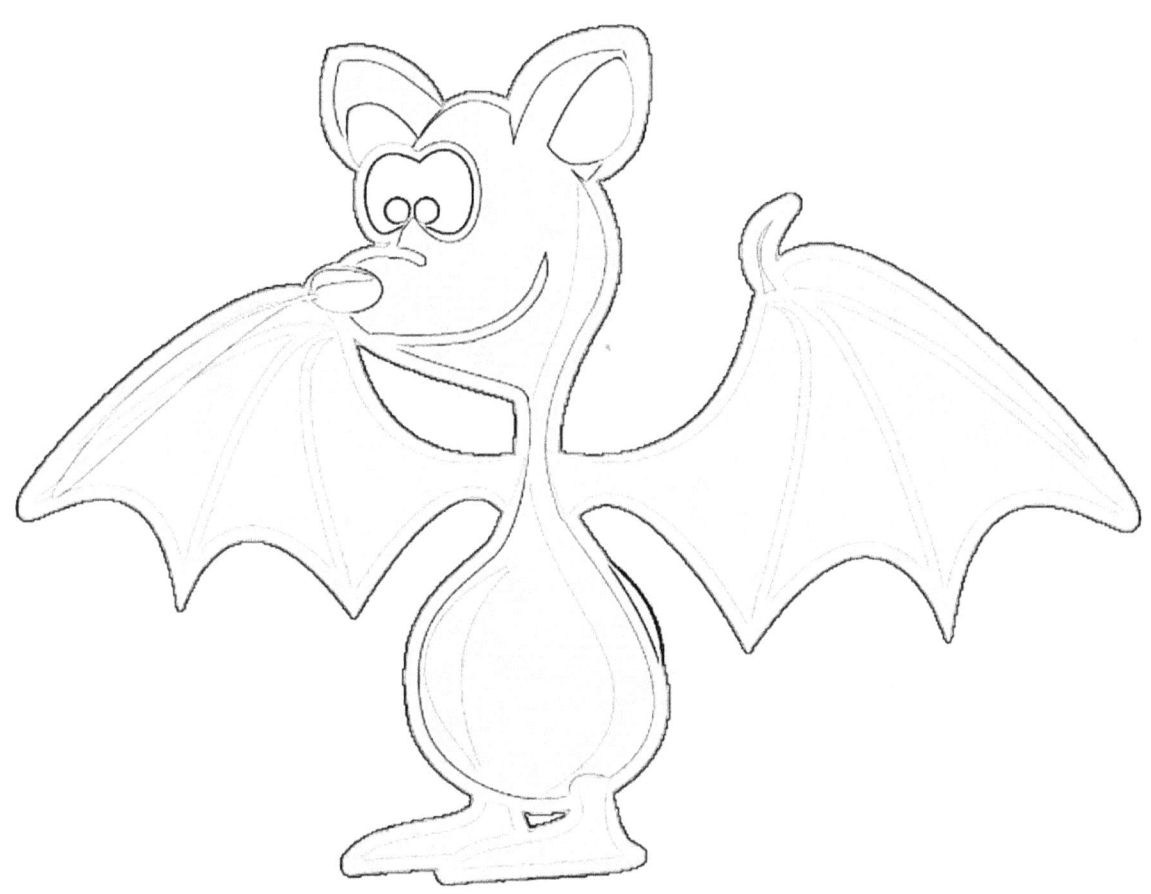

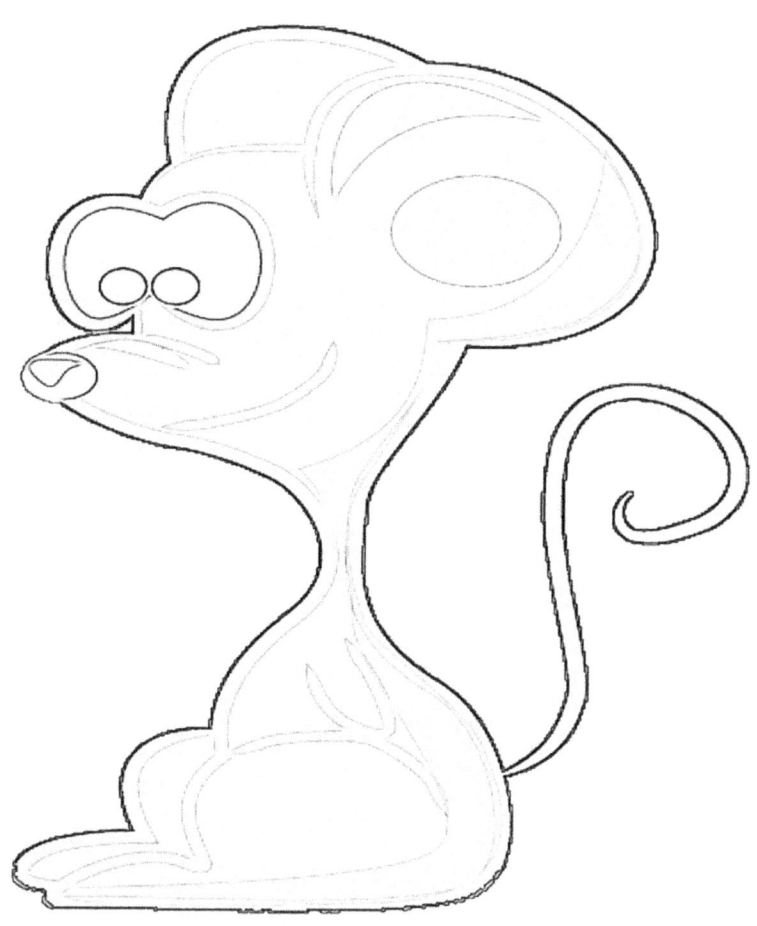

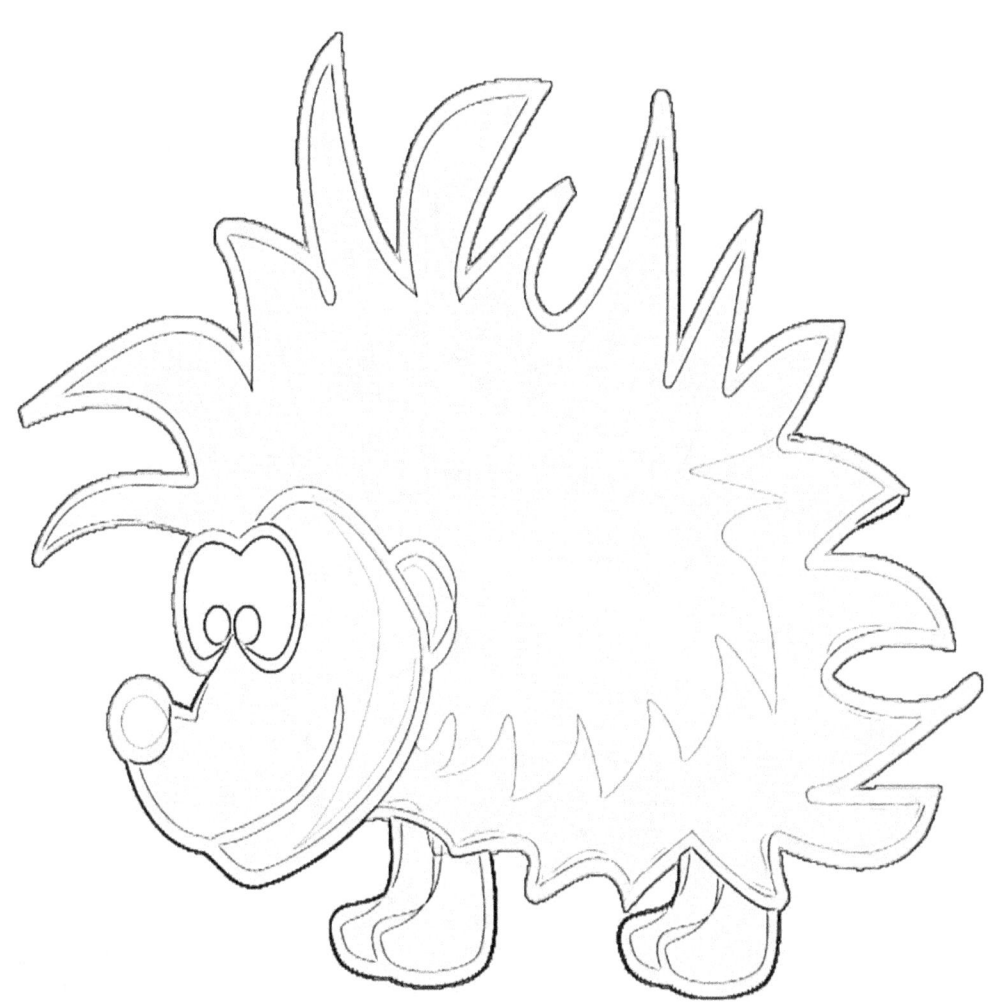

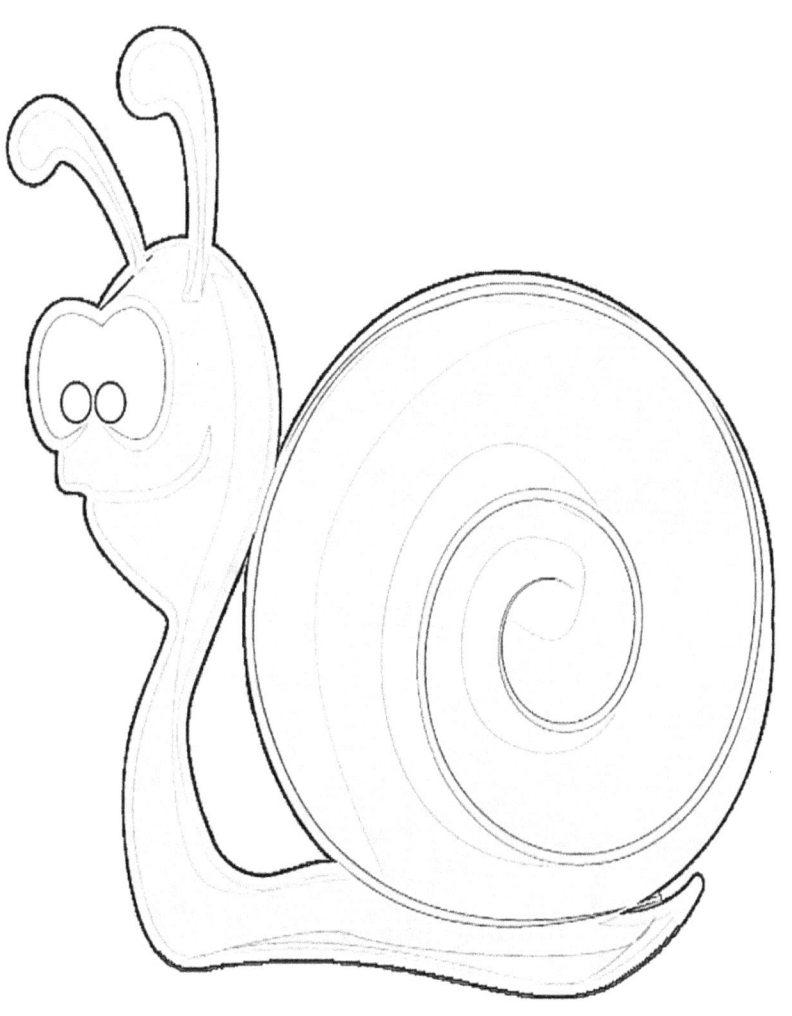

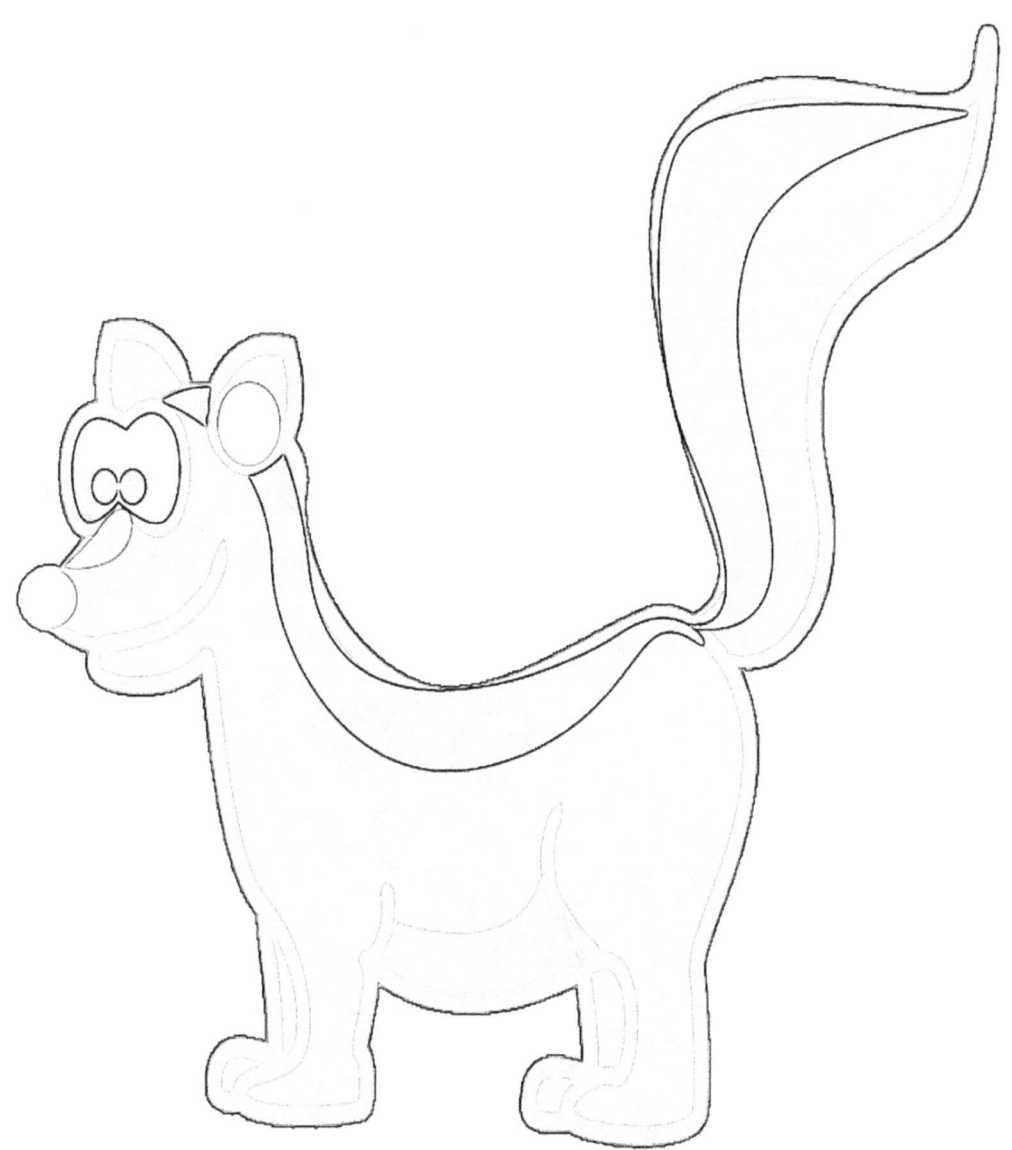

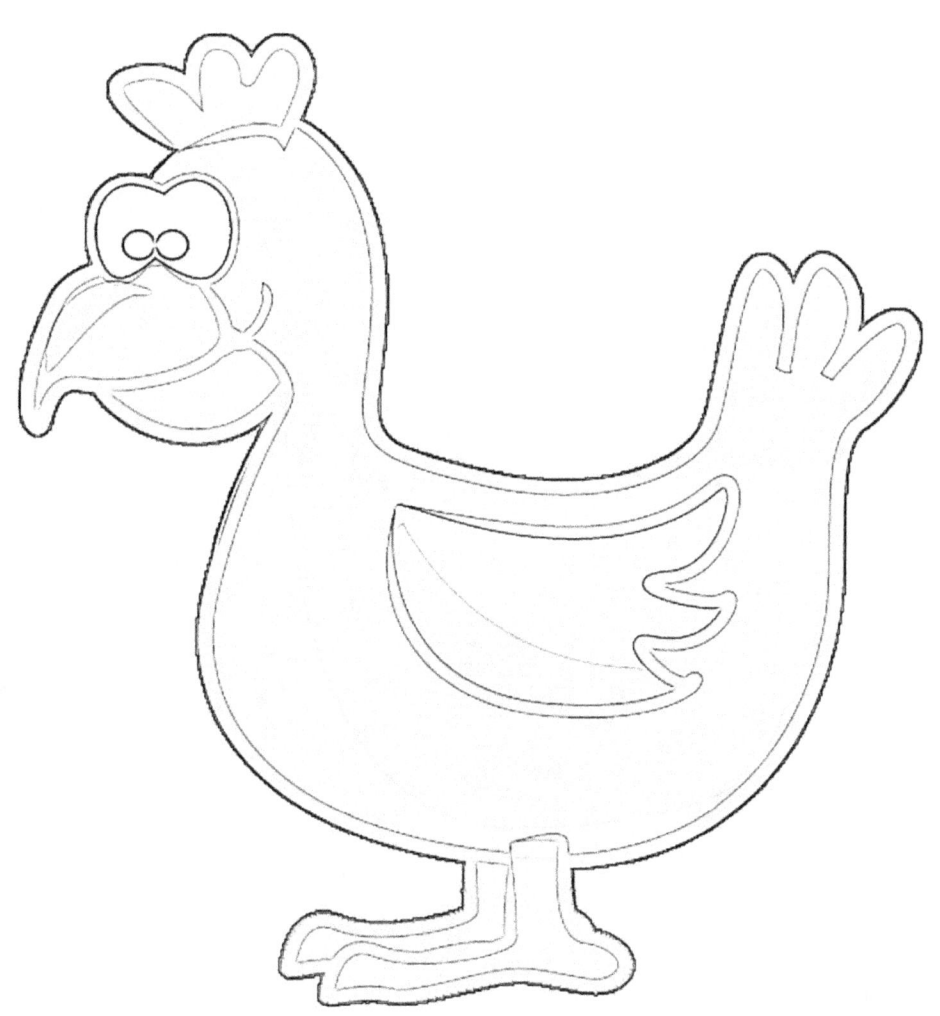

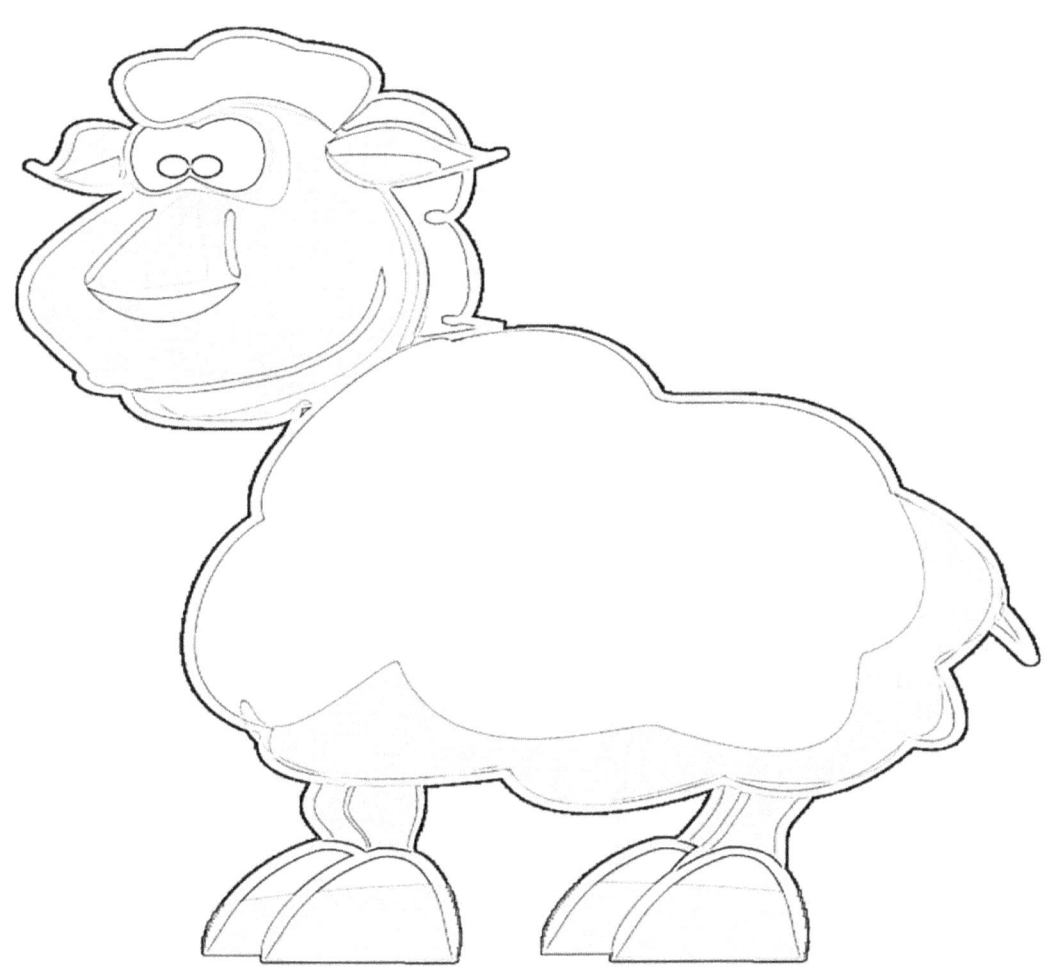

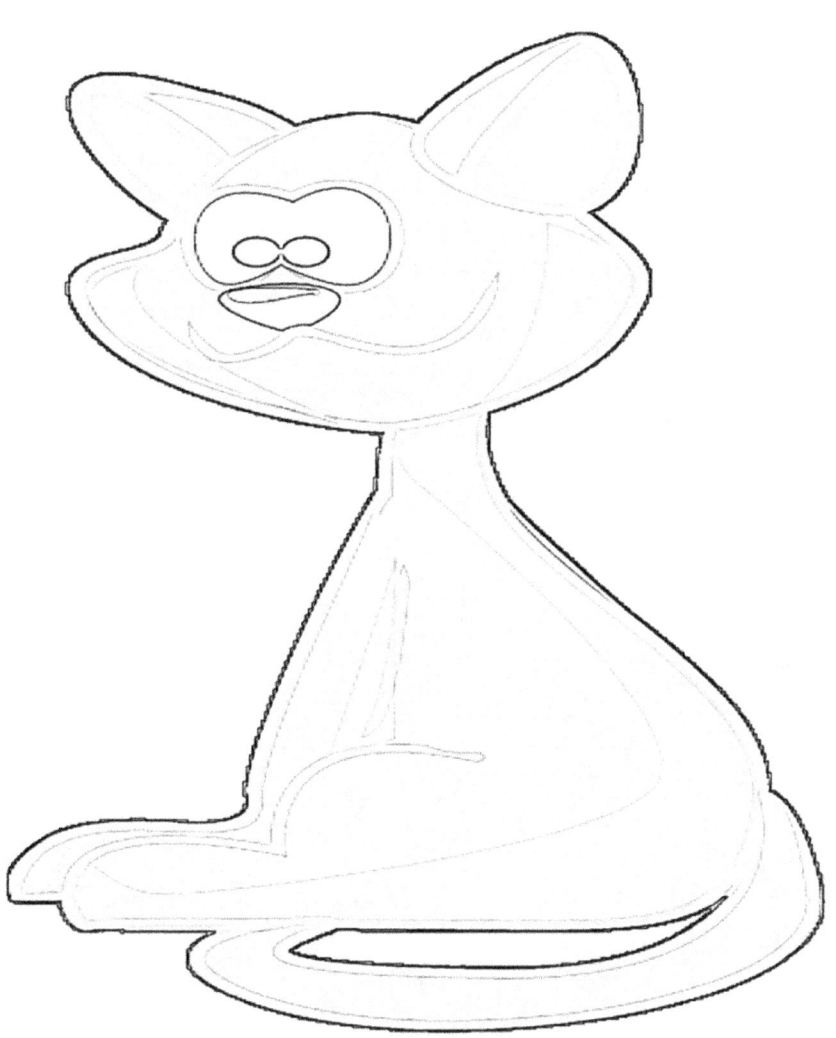

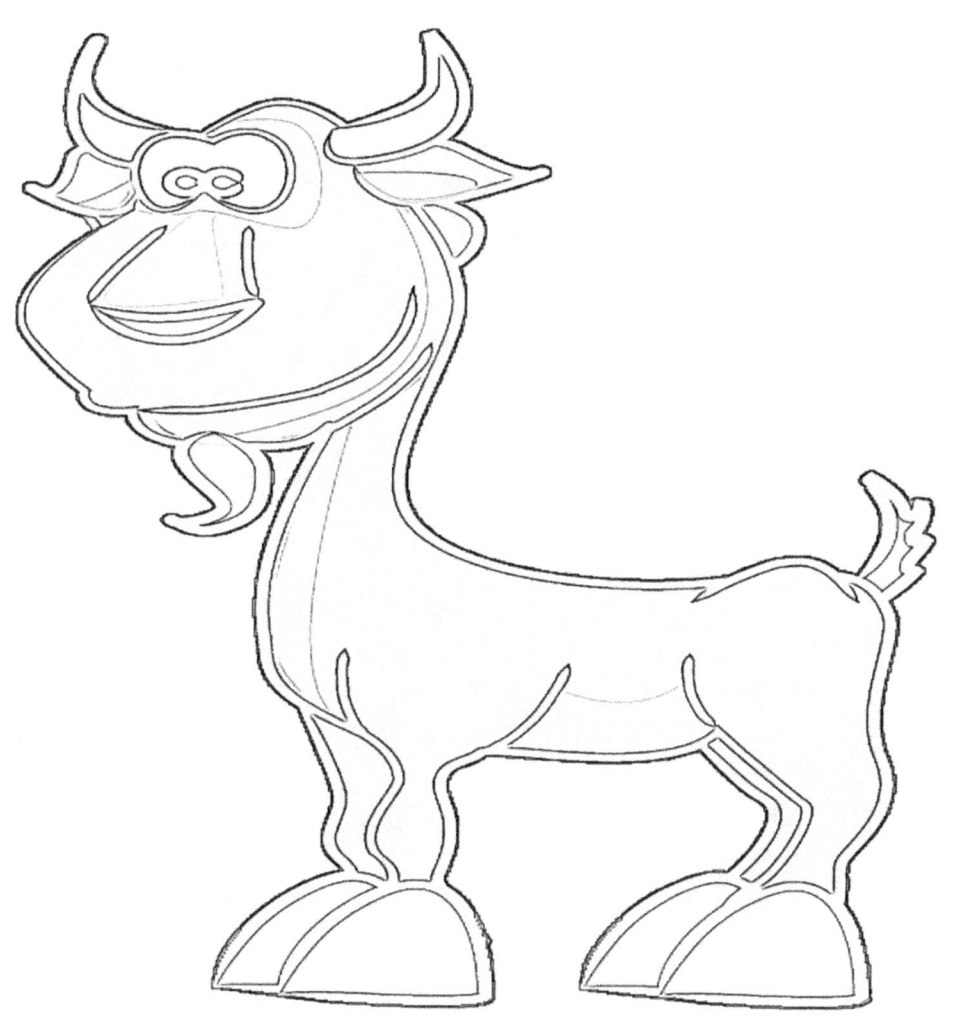

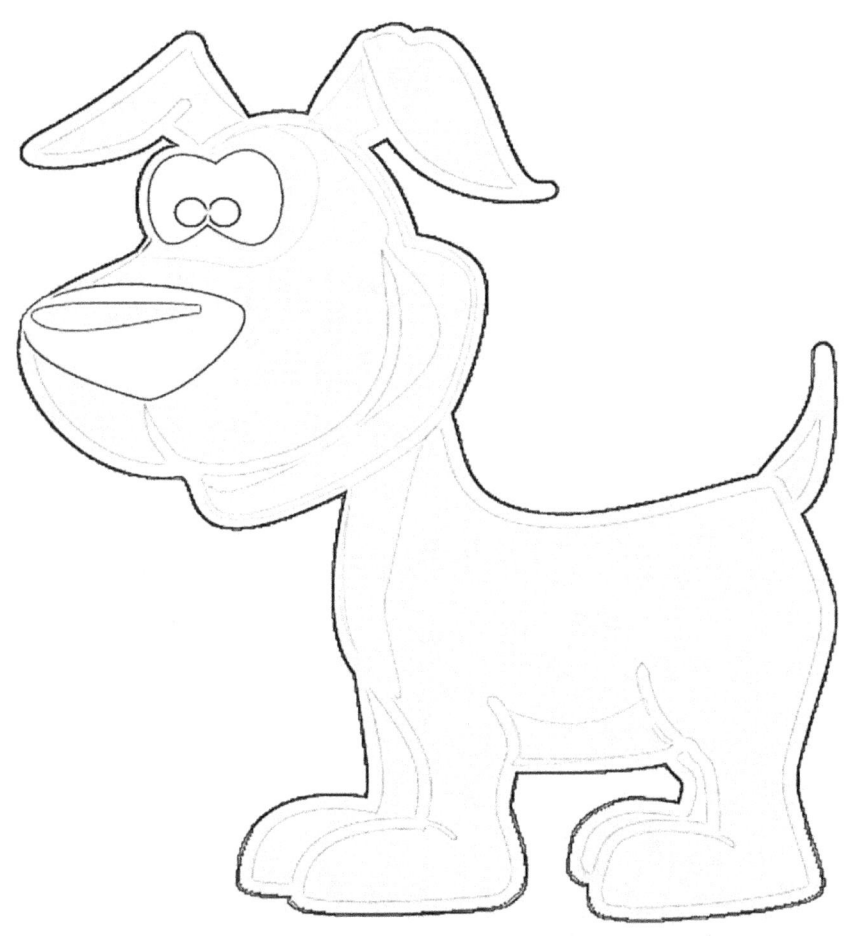

CREATURES of the SEA
Coloring Book

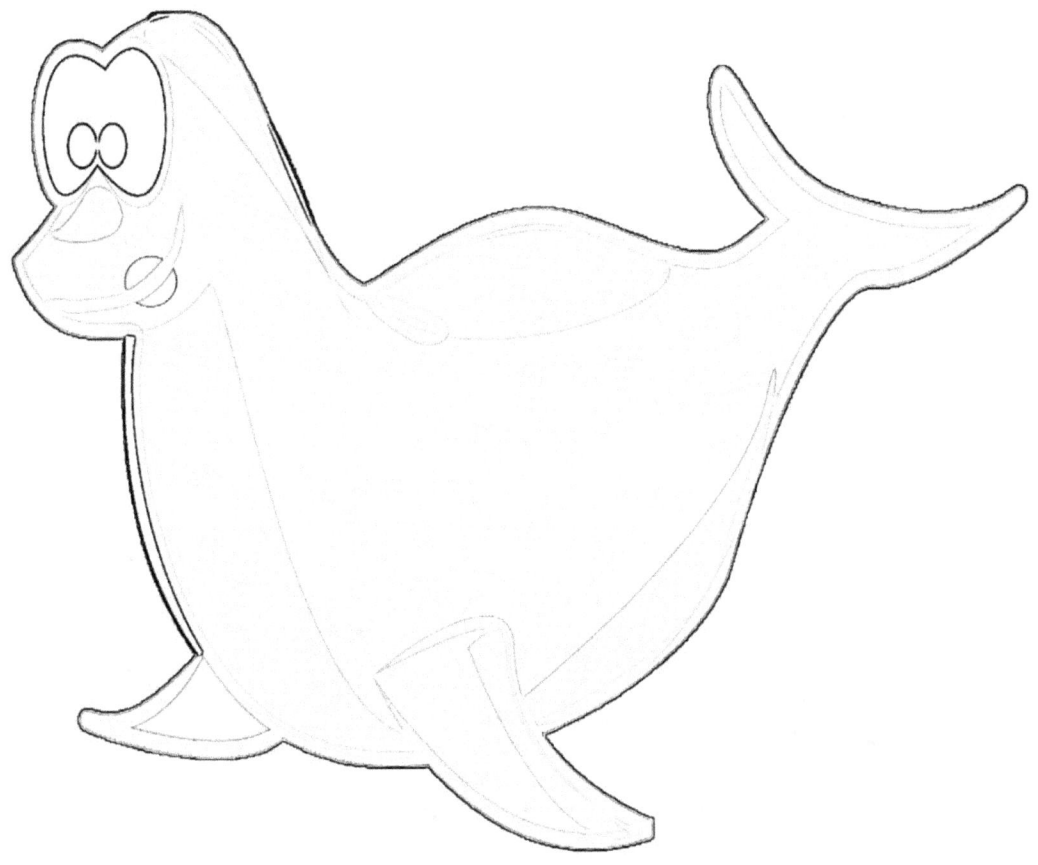

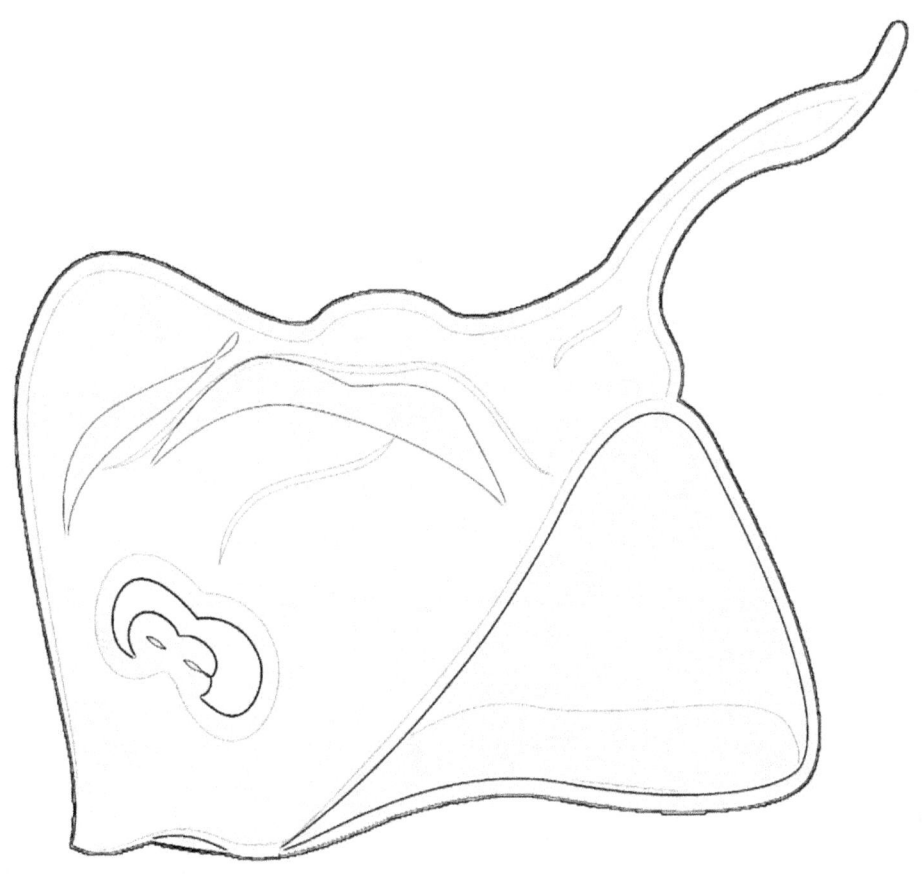

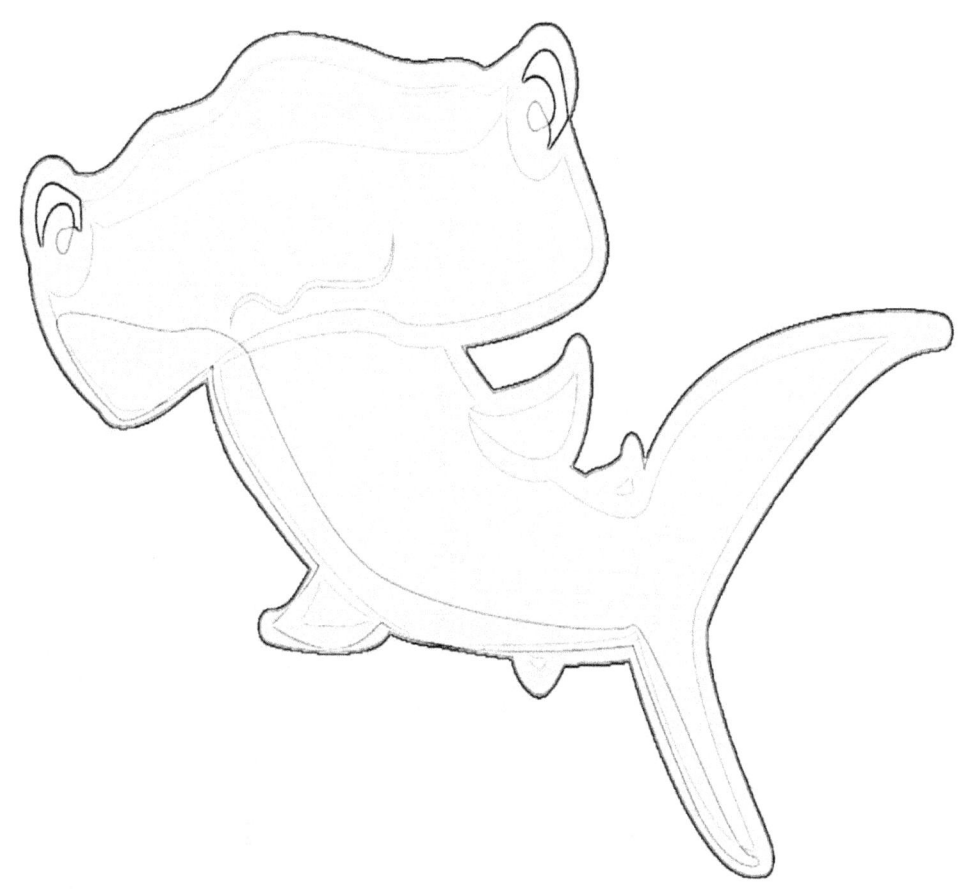

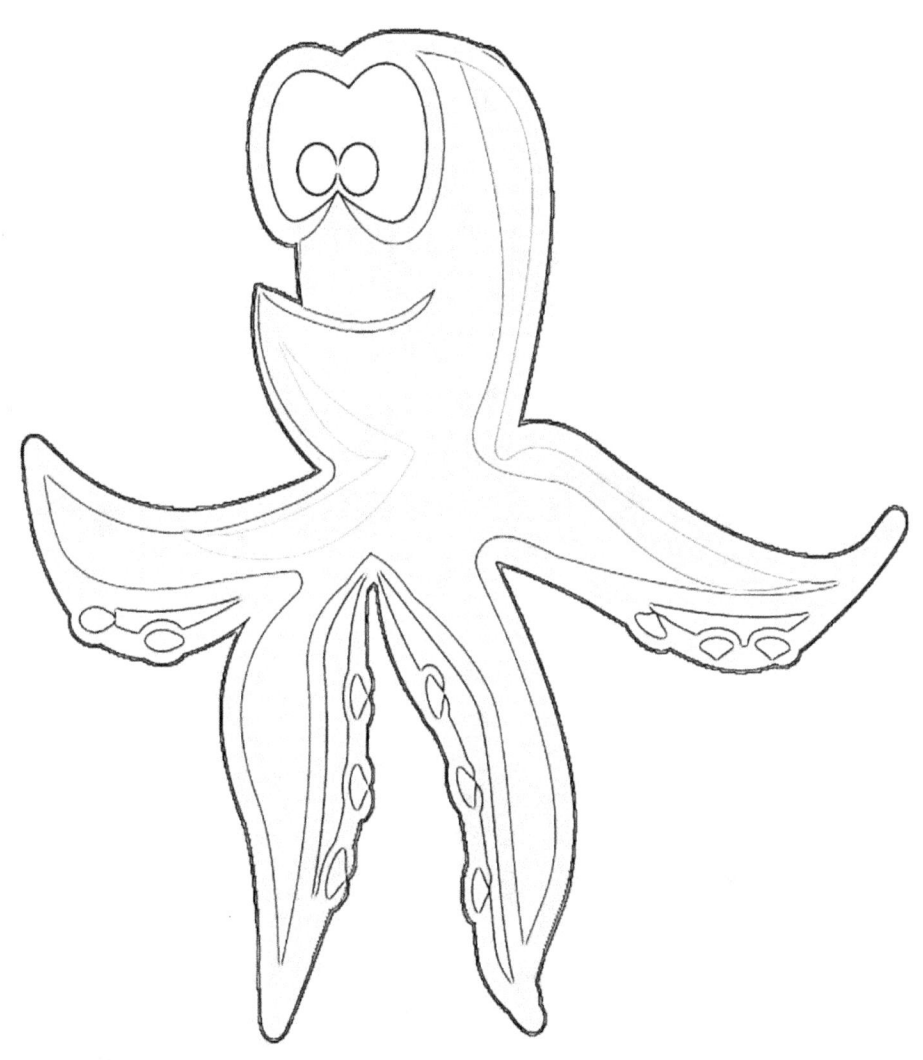

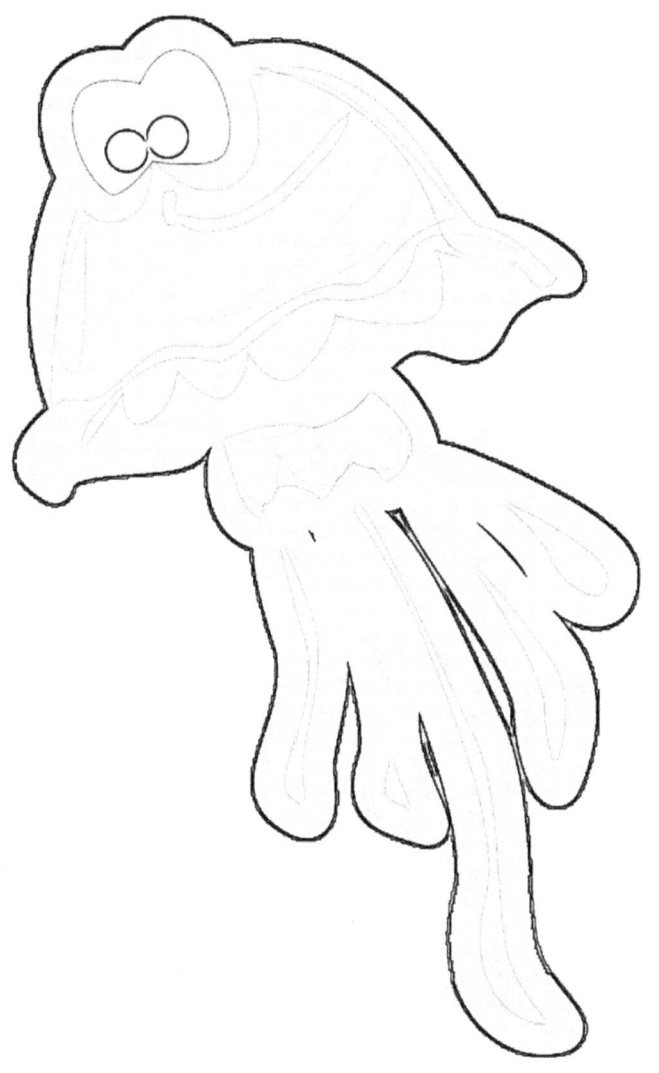

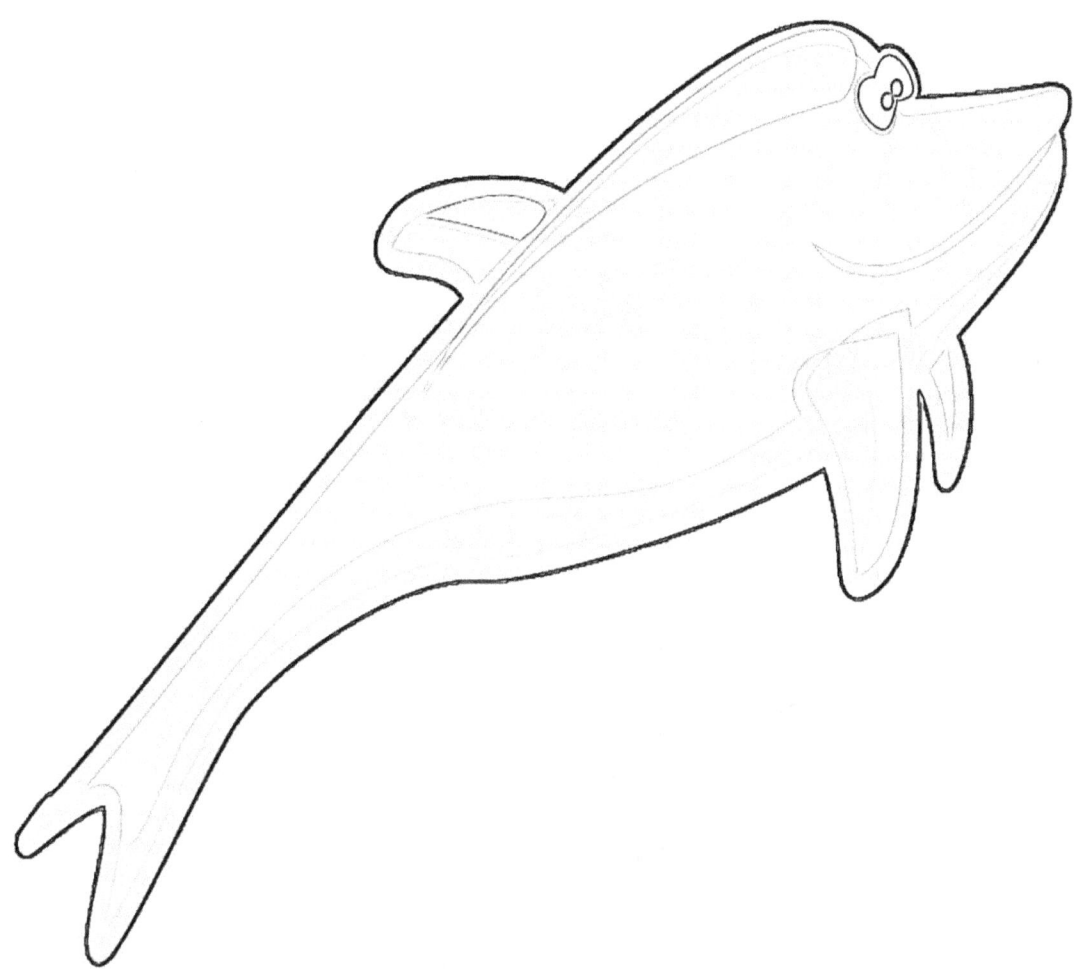

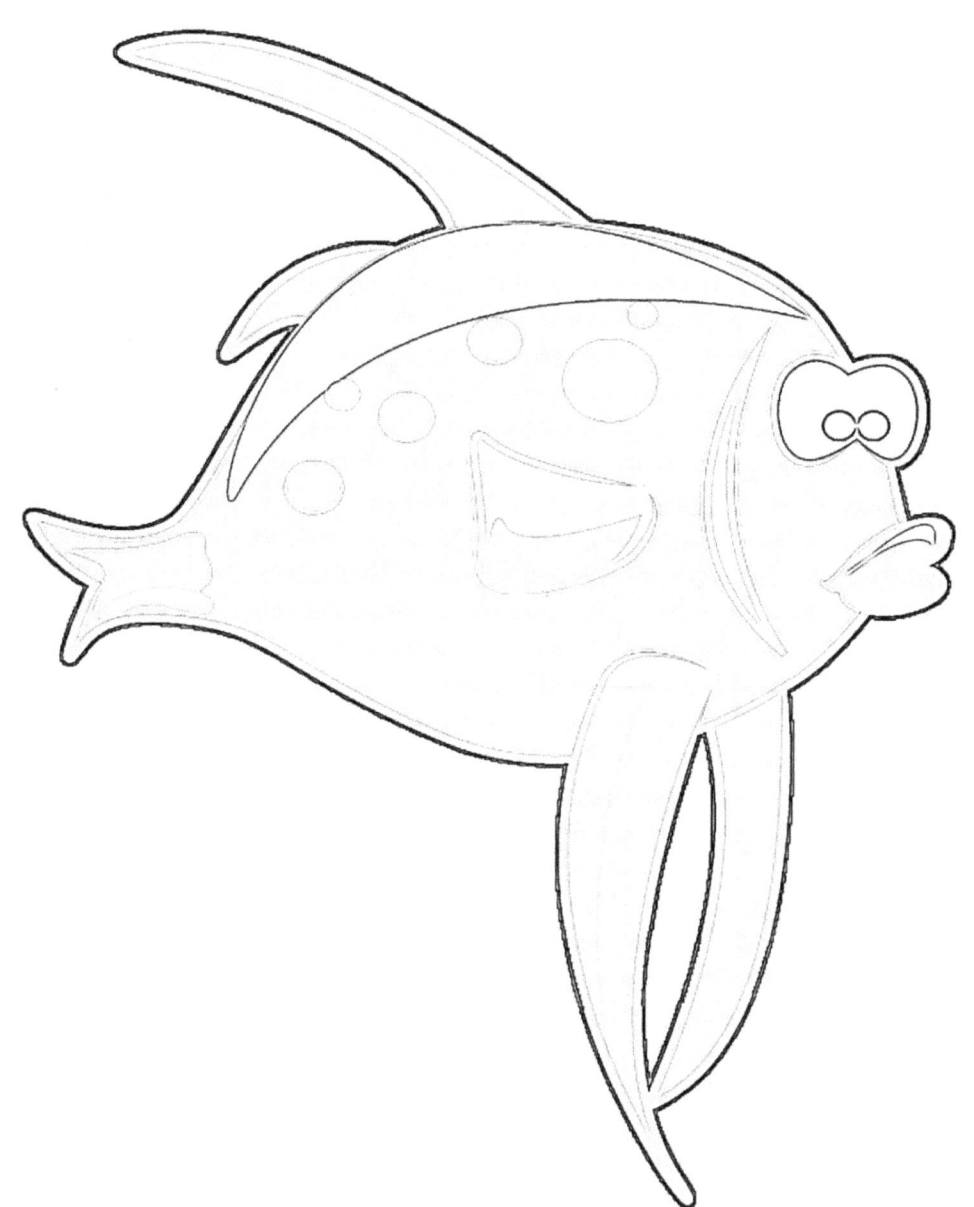

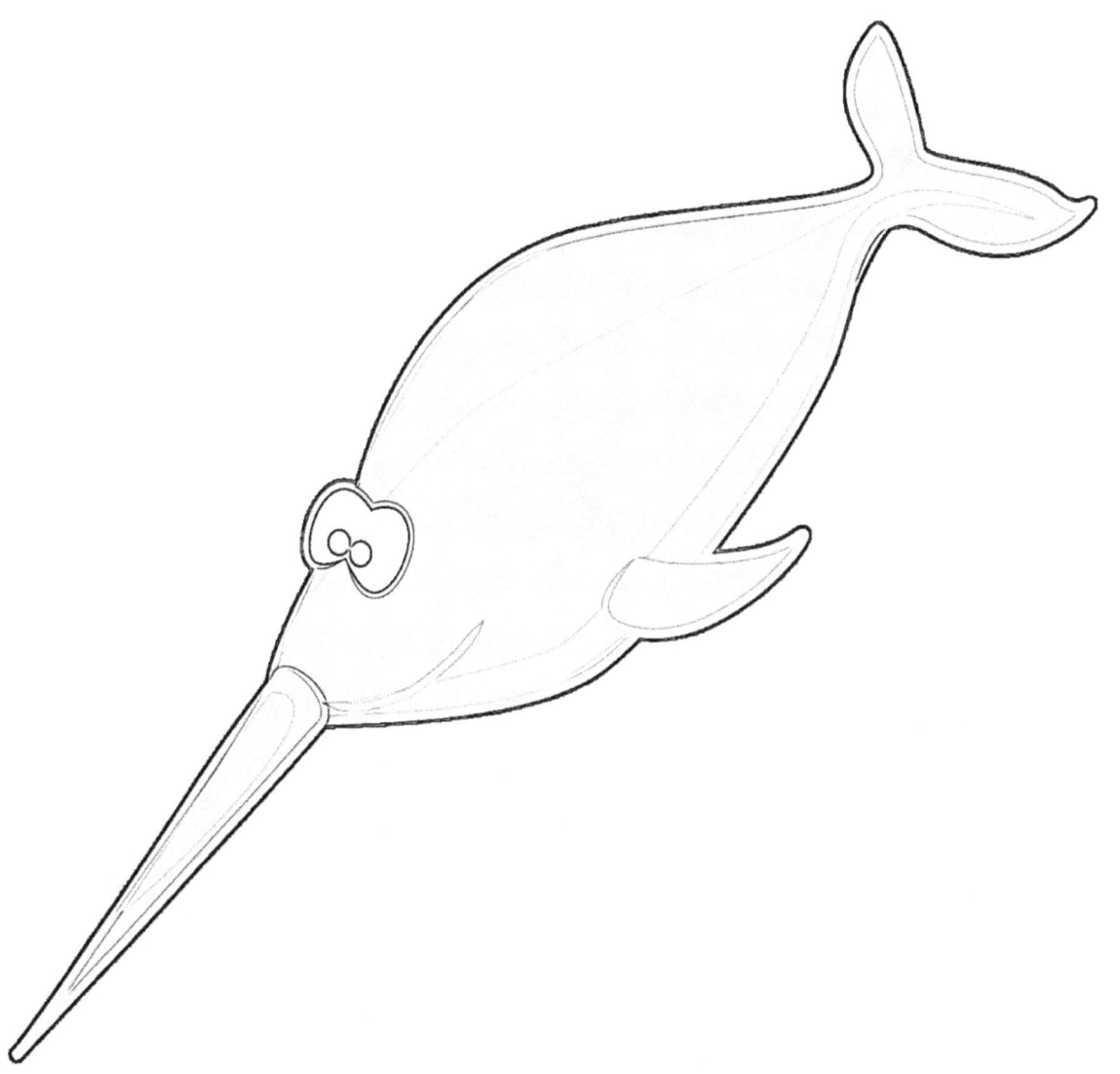

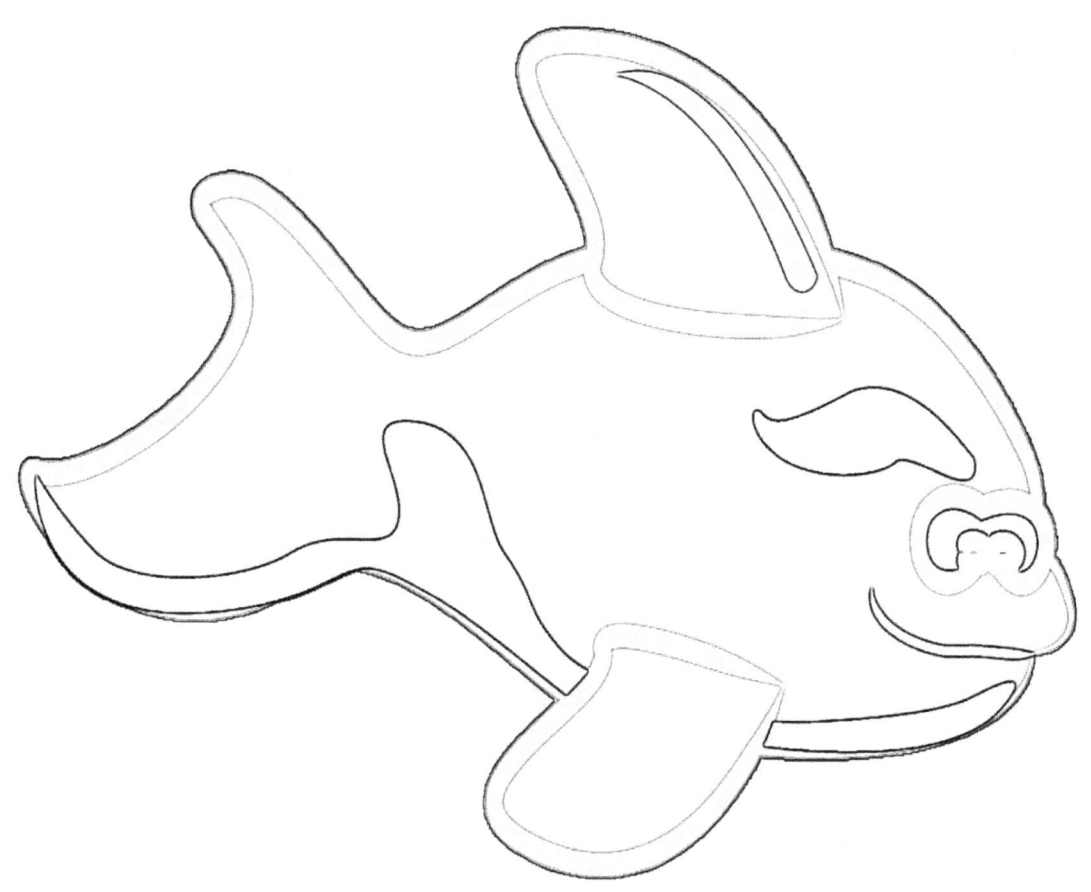

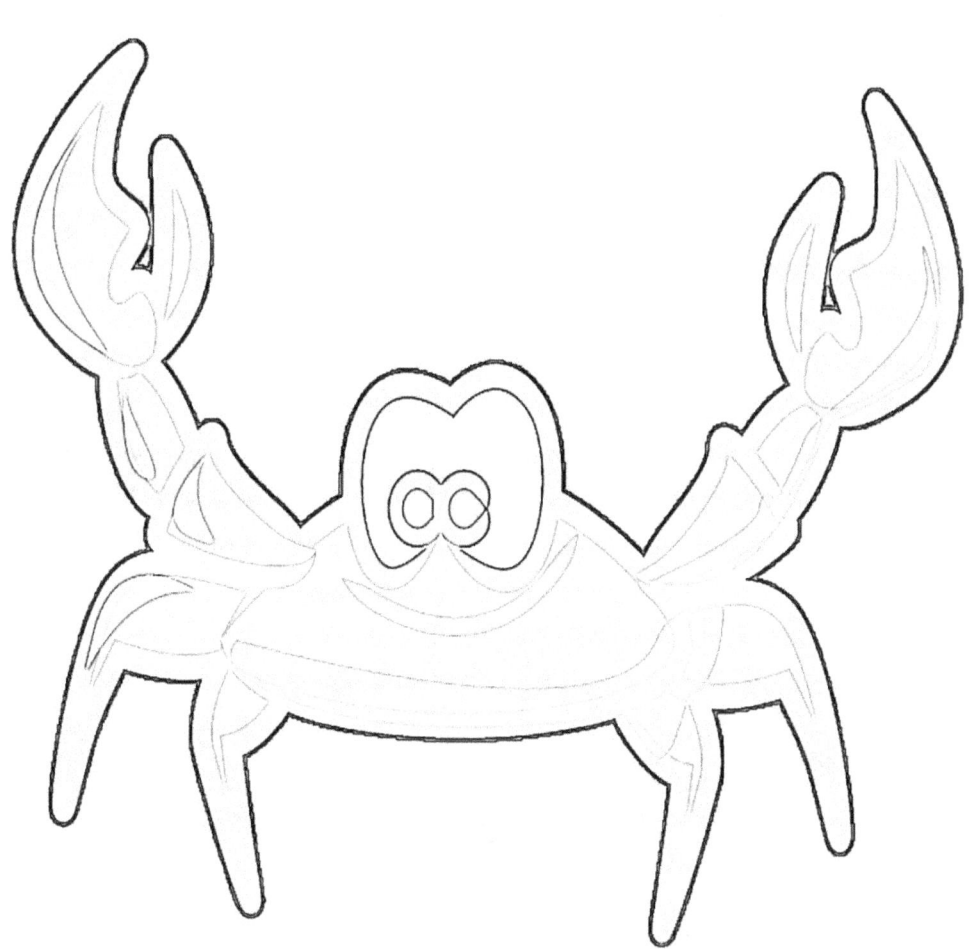

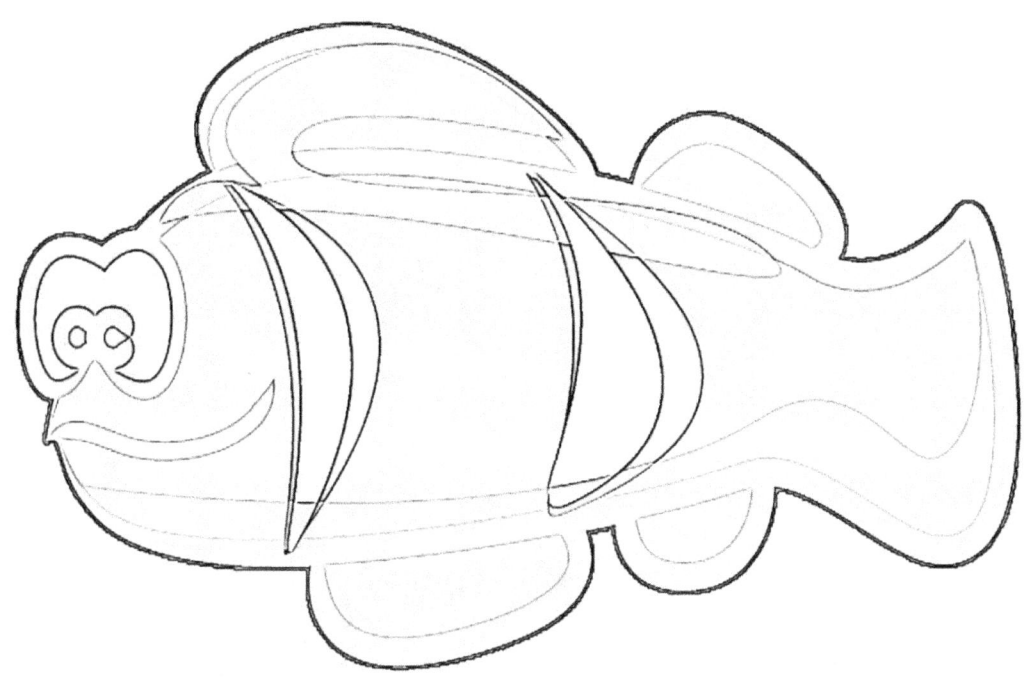

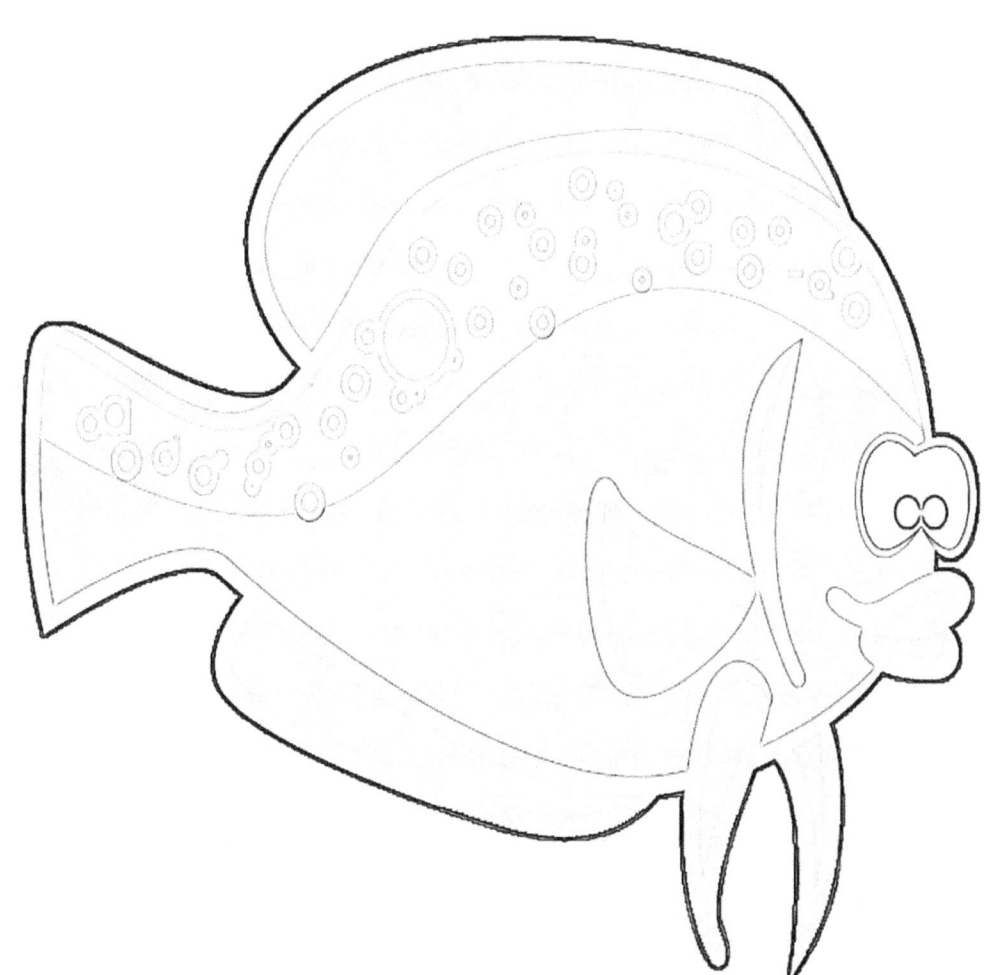

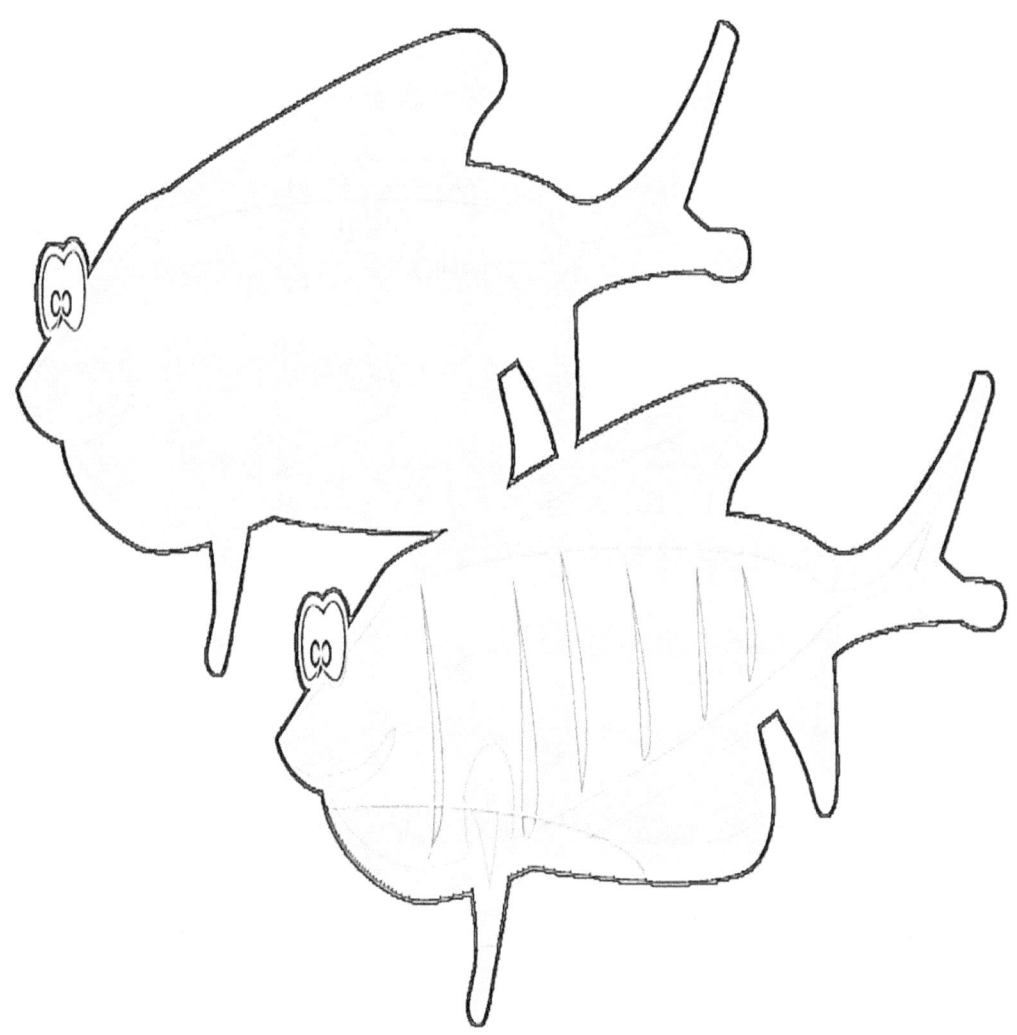

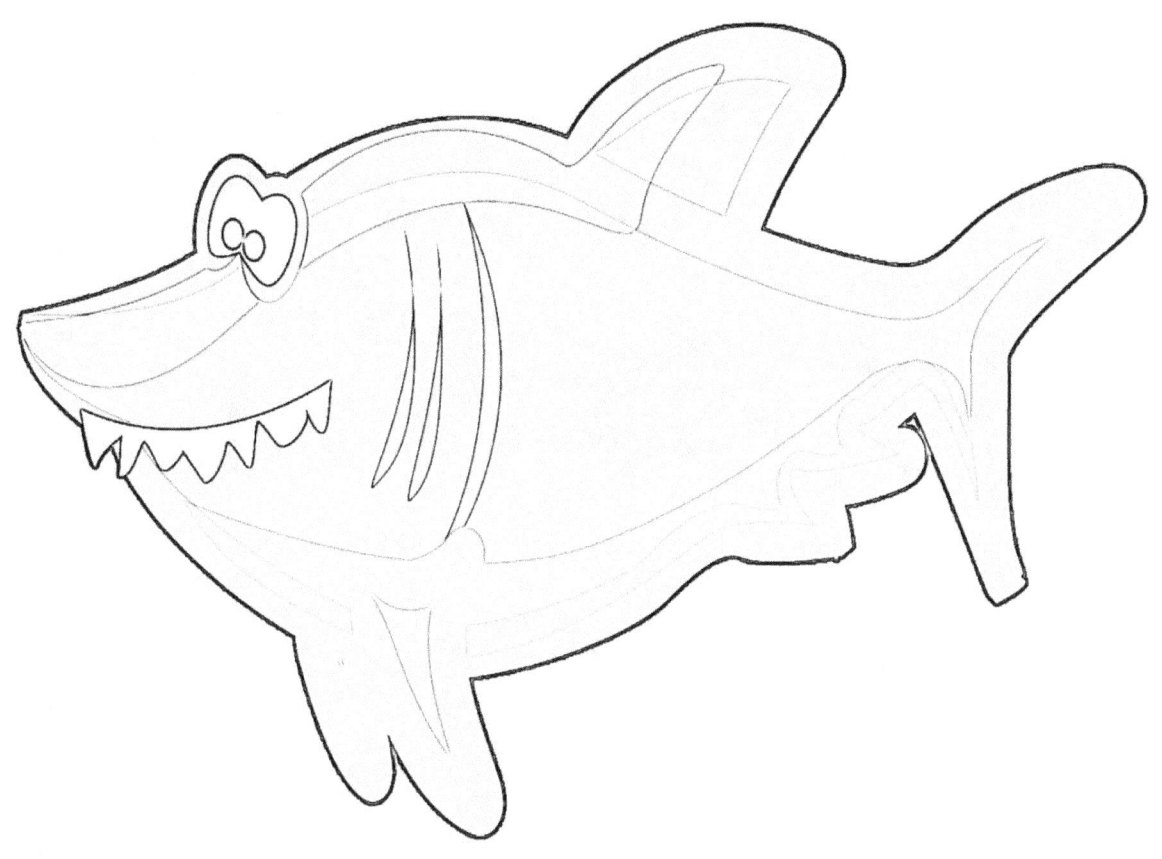

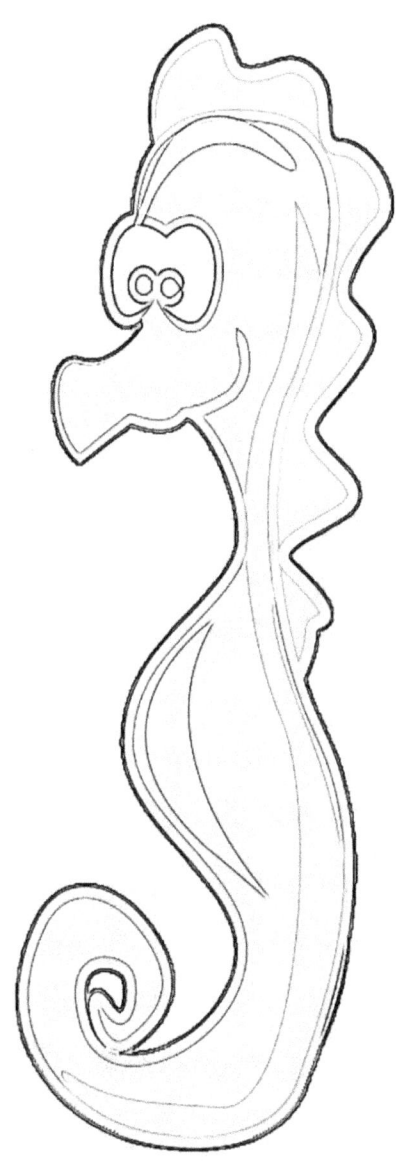

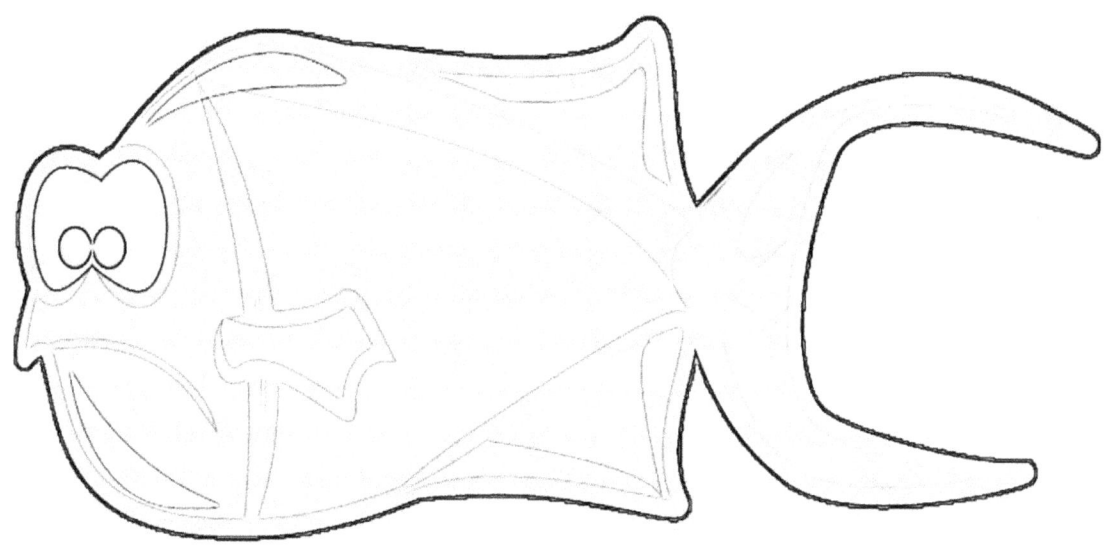

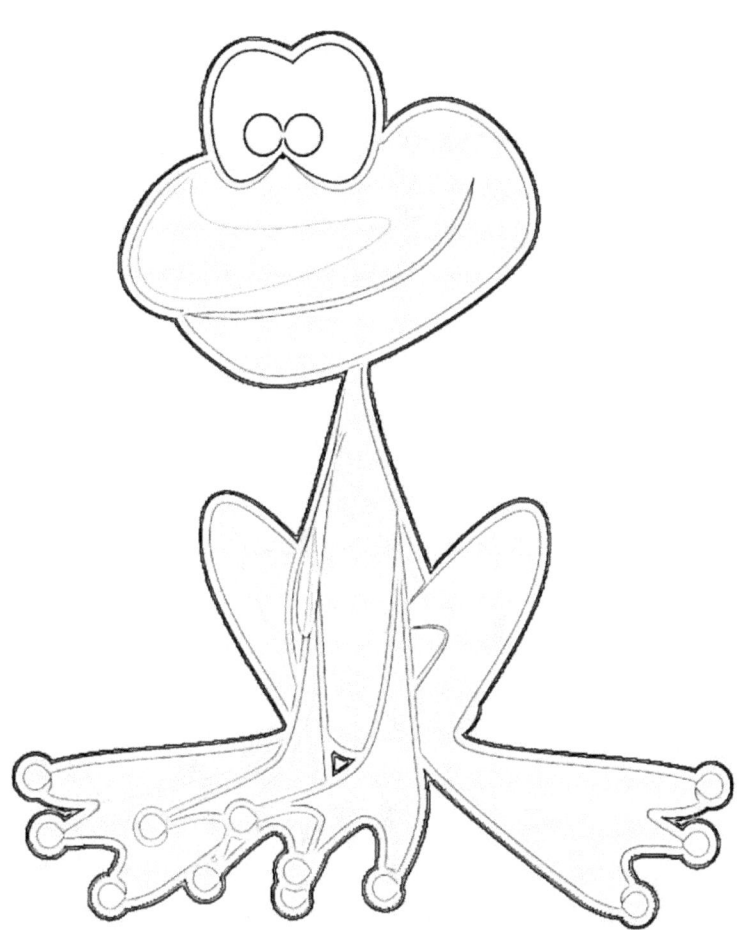

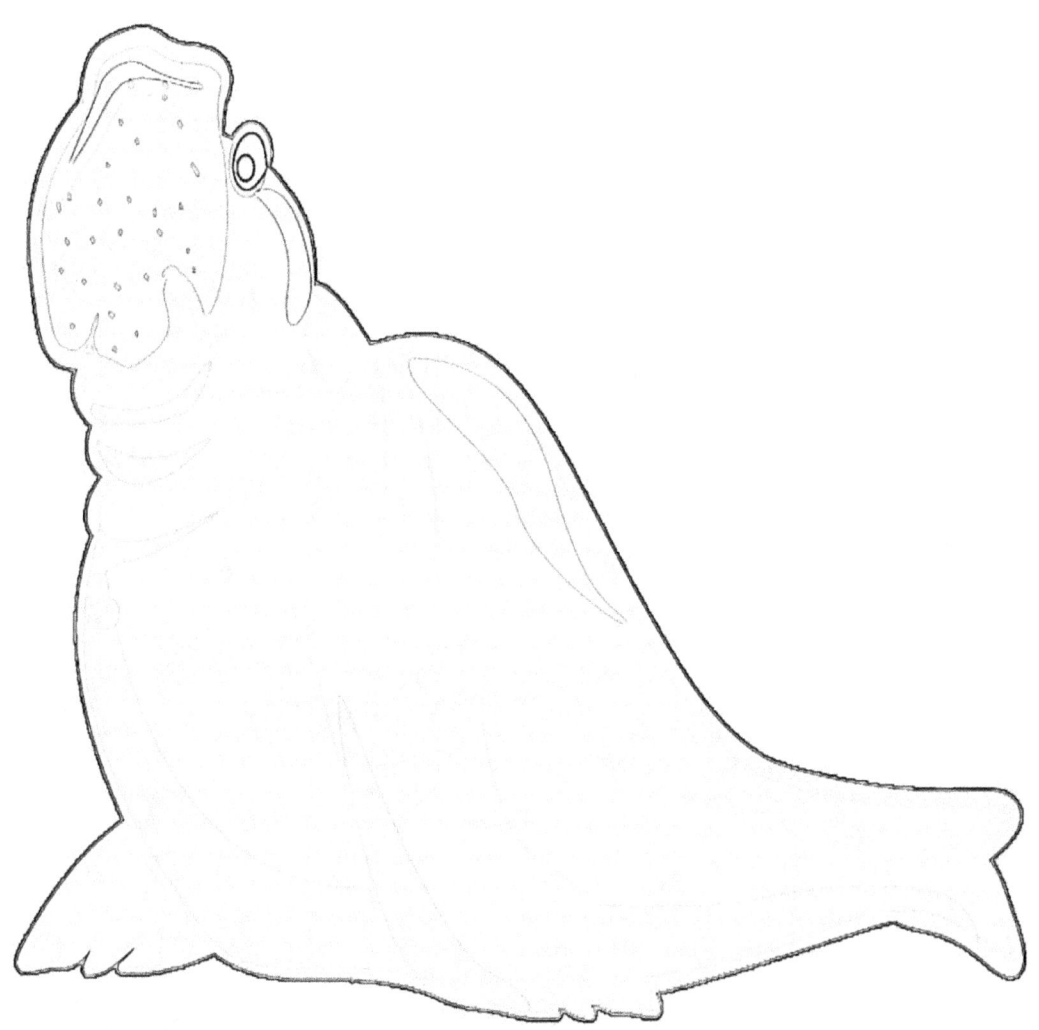

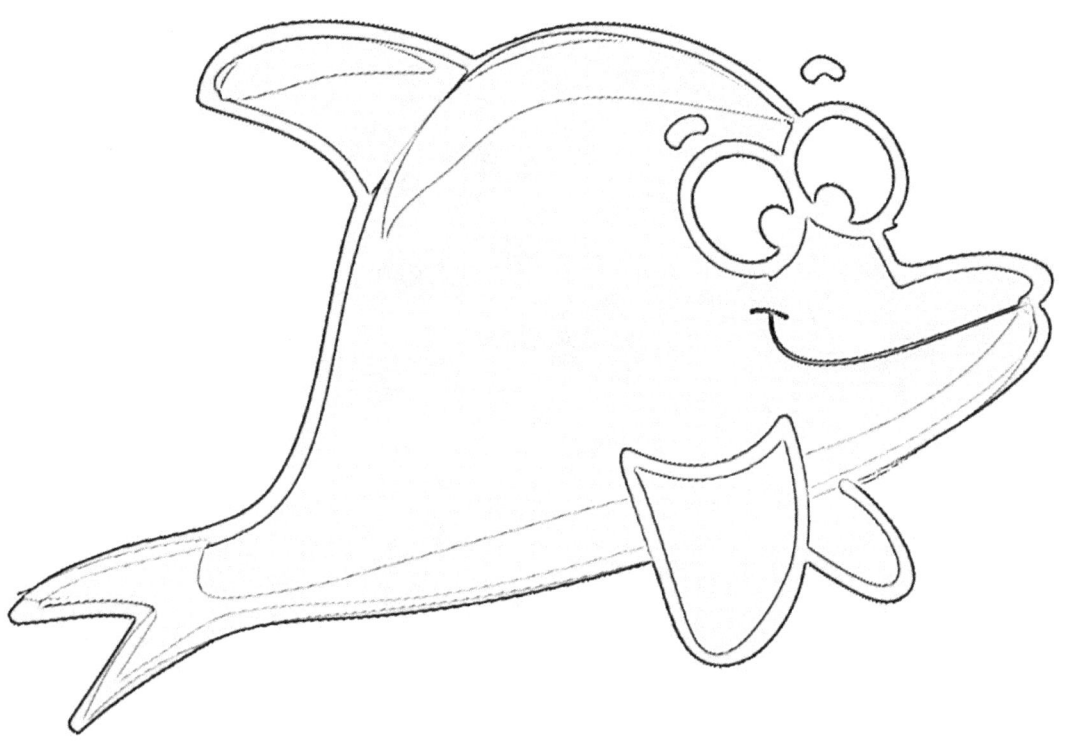

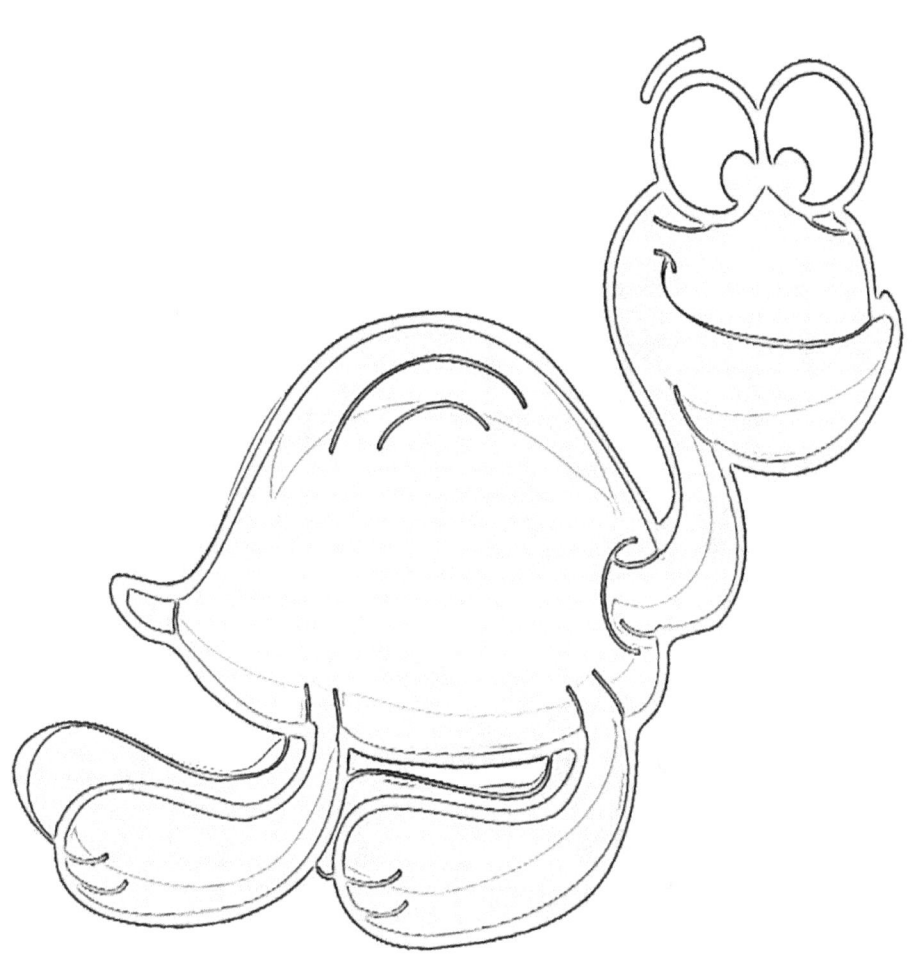

www.ingramcontent.com/pod-product-compliance
Lightning Source LLC
Chambersburg PA
CBHW081554170526
45166CB00009B/2691